Early Praise for *Next-Level A/B Testing*

Next-Level A/B Testing crafts a narrative that brings a range of stakeholders to the table, from QA experts to engineers, and speaks to each of them in their various languages and to their different values. Not only will you come away with a stronger sense of how next-level A/B testing is an iterative, highly collaborative process but you might also find yourself able to communicate with various stakeholders in your organization with better shared language and a deeper understanding of stakeholder values that differ from your own.

➤ **Karl Stolley**
   Software Engineer, Zulip

When time, accuracy, and cost are at the forefront of any engineering effort, teams must build robust testing platforms to increase their efficiency in testing designs, messaging, and back-end configurations. This book will help you level up your testing platform. It introduces you to new A/B testing methods, and you'll also learn how to create good tests that will give you trustworthy data, build systems that can scale, and increase your test data volume.

➤ **Jeana Clark**
   Senior UX Designer and Accessibility Specialist, Civic Tech

Squeeze your A/B testing like never before.

➤ **Jorge Bo**
   Platform Engineer, Hello Fresh

An essential guide to mastering A/B testing—insightful, practical, and indispensable for any data-driven decision-maker.

➤ **Mali Joneanse**
  Software Engineer

This book is a great resource for product managers looking to further their understanding of more advanced A/B testing strategies. It offers practical techniques that improve experimentation beyond the basics, making it an invaluable guide for anyone involved in product experimentation.

➤ **Sonia Namlera**
  Product Manager

Next-Level A/B Testing

Repeatable, Rapid, and Flexible Product Experimentation

Leemay Nassery

The Pragmatic Bookshelf

Dallas, Texas

See our complete catalog of hands-on, practical,
and Pragmatic content for software developers:
https://pragprog.com

Sales, volume licensing, and support:
support@pragprog.com

Derivative works, AI training and testing,
international translations, and other rights:
rights@pragprog.com

The team that produced this book includes:

Publisher: Dave Thomas
COO: Janet Furlow
Executive Editor: Susannah Davidson
Development Editor: Vanya Wryter
Copy Editor: L. Sakhi MacMillan
Indexing: Potomac Indexing, LLC
Layout: Gilson Graphics

ISBN-13: 979-8-88865-130-8
Book version: P1.0—May 2025

Contents

Acknowledgments

To all the reviewers—Bill Gallmeister, Karl Stolley, Uberto Barbini, Jeana Clark, Sonia Namlera, Jorge Bo, Craig Murray, Mali Joneanse, and Stephen Meyer—thank you for your time and energy. Your suggestions helped make this book better.

To my development editor, Vanya Wryter, and the entire Pragmatic team—this is our second book together! Thank you for your kindness and support.

Finally, thank you to my family and friends for your unwavering support and love. I considered making an experimentation joke here—something about living life with the blind confidence of a year-long holdback likely to get invalidated—but the truth is, I just want to say thank you.

Introduction

Let's say you're already familiar with the basics of A/B testing, like defining hypotheses, success metrics, and variants, from reading my first book, *Practical A/B Testing*. In that book, you learned about the basic anatomy of an A/B test, how to foster a culture of experimentation, and the essential elements needed to run an experiment on a product.

Now, you've moved beyond those initial stages. You're running experiments weekly, gaining insights into user engagement, and launching features based on those results. Your engineering and product teams see the value of evaluating features through experiments, making A/B testing a standard part of your product development process. Overall, the culture of experimentation has become deeply engrained in your company.

But with this success comes new challenges. Perhaps you're looking to run more experiments simultaneously to increase your testing velocity and unblock teams that would otherwise face delays. Maybe you've encountered frustrating experiment restarts due to misconfigurations, highlighting the need for more thorough validation processes.

If any of this is relatable, then you're in the right place! In this book, you'll learn how to elevate your experimentation practices, developing techniques to enhance A/B testing rate, cost efficiency, and quality.

Who Should Read This Book

This book assumes you have experience running A/B tests on user-facing products. You could be a product manager, a software engineer, a business analyst, an engineering manager, or any role in between.

If you're a data scientist, you'll likely already be familiar with a good portion of experimentation strategies detailed in this book, but you would benefit from the practical lens of enabling each experimentation strategy on a platform.

Now if you're new to the experimentation domain, read *Practical A/B Testing* first to become familiar with the anatomy of an A/B test before reading this book.

Simplifying Complex Concepts

The primary goal of this book, beyond helping you improve your experimentation practices, is to break down the more advanced concepts into simple, actionable terms. By doing so, you'll gain the context and confidence needed to apply these strategies in your own work.

Since this book is designed to be accessible to nonexperts in the experimentation field, the strategies are often paired with relatable metaphors—like cooking or running—that make the ideas easier to grasp. These analogies aim to bridge the gap between complex techniques and practical application, ensuring that the core principles are approachable for everyone. This book is written in a way that lets you skip around and not have to read each chapter in order.

How This Book Is Organized

This book offers practical strategies to improve A/B testing rate, cost, and quality on a product. Specifically, we'll cover these topics in the following chapters:

- *Chapter 1.* The rationale for improving experimentation rate, cost, and quality.
- *Chapter 2.* The strategies for running more experiments in parallel.
- *Chapter 3.* The factors to consider when configuring a well-designed and effective experiment.
- *Chapter 4.* The various experimentation tactics to enable machine learning evaluations.
- *Chapter 5.* The monitoring and validation techniques to ensure quality experiments.
- *Chapter 6.* The tactics to ensure trustworthy data insights.
- *Chapter 7.* The common adaptive testing strategies.
- *Chapter 8.* The cost of long-term holdbacks and how to adapt.
- *Chapter 9.* The key factors for deciding when to make tradeoffs.

You'll find Engineer Tasks and a Chapter Roundup to practice the concepts within each chapter. Don't skip the tasks and chapter roundups! Completing these exercises will prepare you to practice what you've learned in the real world at your company.

For each Engineer Task, you'll play the role of an engineer on a team at a fictitious company, MarketMax, that has been running A/B tests on its website for years. However, as the company and product have scaled, they're now running into coordination constraints, quality issues, and engineering cost concerns. You'll gain experience and understanding through practical hands-on engineering tasks that effectively address common problems teams face after they've surpassed the beginning stages of running experiments in production.

Online Resources

You can always visit the book's official web page[1] to participate in discussions on the book's forum and review the latest updates and errata on DevTalk.[2]

Taking Your Experimentation to the Next Level

The long-term success of using A/B testing to innovate and evolve a product hinges on the robustness of your experimentation practices. When you invest in your experimentation strategies, you're directly influencing the speed and quality of decisions made on a product. The better tools you have in your experimentation tool kit, the better off teams will be shipping and evaluating new features on a product. That's what this book is all about.

Let's jump right in!

---

1. https://pragprog.com/titles/abtestprac/next-level-a-b-testing/
2. https://devtalk.com/books/next-level-a-b-testing/

CHAPTER 1

Why Experimentation Rate, Quality, and Cost Matter

Product experiences that were A/B tested are all around you. Have you watched a show on a streaming app? If so, the UX was very likely evaluated in an online experiment. Have you browsed an e-commerce site or scrolled through a social media app? If so, the algorithms recommending content to you were absolutely A/B tested for effectiveness. Practicing A/B testing can transform good products into great ones, while enabling engineering, design, and product teams to truly understand the impact of their changes and features on the product.

While a product may undergo significant changes to meet the needs of its users and business, your experimentation practices, which are used to test and validate these changes, should evolve as well. If the experimentation strategies you employ stagnate, you risk delaying product decisions or having testing become a bottleneck that limits the speed and quality of iterations made to a product. Taking your experimentation practices to the next level so you continue to gain insights as the product evolves is critical to ensuring A/B testing remains a first-class step in the product development life cycle.

This book builds on the fundamentals from *Practical A/B Testing* by exploring three critical areas that will take your experimentation strategies to the next level: experimentation rate, quality, and cost. In this chapter, we'll explore the pivotal experimentation stages and how they align with these focus areas. Let's get into it!

Advancing Your Experimentation Practices

Let's say you like to cook every night. You usually use a knife and various utensils to slice, dice, and construct your meal. Over time, you notice you're cooking less because your tools are outdated, don't necessarily meet the needs of a meal's advanced cooking techniques, or have dulled, making them unusable. Because you value the many benefits of cooking at home, you invest in new tools to maintain your track record of creating healthy meals by purchasing a nonstick skillet, slow cooker, and food processor. With these new tools, you're ready to take your meals to the next level.

Practicing A/B testing is similar to this cooking scenario. If your experimentation practices don't evolve alongside the innovations in your product, you risk skipping this crucial step in the product development life cycle. As a result, you may miss out on the valuable insights gained from evaluating changes through an A/B test, making it harder to understand the true impact of product updates.

Successfully evaluating product changes with online controlled experiments (A/B tests) relies on a strong engineering platform. Every A/B test follows a series of essential steps: defining a clear hypothesis, choosing the right success and guardrail metrics to measure impact, and analyzing the data to drive product decisions. These steps can be grouped into three key categories:

1. Experiment design
2. Experiment execution
3. Experiment analysis

The image shown on page 3 outlines the specific steps that fall under each category.

When A/B testing is a key step in your product development life cycle, there's always room for improvement—whether it's increasing your platform's throughput, improving the quality of insights, or adopting new techniques to improve success rates. As you reflect on the capabilities already built into your experimentation platform, you likely are also thinking of the gaps that hinder running A/B tests smoothly. These gaps, or opportunities, become increasingly complex as your experimentation practices evolve and enable many teams across many distinct areas of a product.

For instance, your main challenge might be getting reliable metrics in place—turning a chaotic sea of data into a smooth-running insights engine. Once you've got that sorted and built a solid metrics platform, the next challenge could be creating a self-service application that lets teams set up

Experiment Design

Step 1: UX designers, product managers, or engineers have an idea for an experiment influenced by data or user research.

Step 2: Design the experiment; create a hypothesis, success metrics, power analysis, etc.

Step 3: Validate experiment configuration via a clear QA process, verifying each variant is configured correctly.

Experiment Execution

Step 4: Launch the experiment to a subset of users.

Step 5: Actively monitor to ensure there are no errors or serious degradation in the user experience.

Step 6: End the experiment; ensure all the necessary steps to properly disable the control and test variants are followed and metrics were powered sufficiently.

Experiment Analysis

Step 7: Analyze results.

Step 8: Share results with key stakeholders and partner teams.

Step 9: Decide on whether to launch, retest, or use the insights to influence future experiments on the product.

experiments effortlessly with just a few clicks. Or maybe the focus shifts to scaling your platform so it can handle more experiments running at the same time with ease.

One of the defining characteristics of A/B testing is that it requires collaboration across multiple disciplines. Four key roles are typically involved in running well-designed, effective experiments: a product owner to define the hypothesis and align it with business goals; a UX designer to propose user-centered design changes and contribute insights from user research; a data scientist to guide statistical decisions such as power analysis and the selection of success and guardrail metrics; and an engineer to manage the infrastructure and systems that support the test. This cross-functional approach makes A/B testing a complex process—one that demands a blend of technical, analytical, design, and collaborative skills to execute well.

Illustrating Common Challenges

Given its complexity, the more efficient your experimentation practices are, the more likely teams will use the methodology to evaluate new ideas. The more time intensive it is to orchestrate an A/B test, the less likely teams will incorporate this step into their product development process. Depending on where you are in your experimentation journey, you're either focusing on scaling certain capabilities or improving specific steps within the end-to-end process.

Check out the following image for an illustration of the typical progression and the challenges you'll face as you take your experimentation practices to the next level.

	Beginner	Advanced Beginner	Intermediate	Advanced Intermediate	Advanced
Description	The initial experimentation platform has been built but most steps to enable an A/B test on a product are manual.	The core steps in the testing process are self-service, but certain tasks, like adding new metrics, still require significant engineering effort.	The platform team is hyper-focused on scaling and improving the testing process with better tooling and test design strategies.	The key problem spaces revolve around specific domain areas such as accelerating ML evaluations and improving quality of insights.	The investment areas include variance reduction strategies and methodologies to gain insights with either fewer users or shorter durations.
Primary Experimentation Challenge	Building momentum and desire for A/B testing versus skipping this key step in the product development life cycle.	Increasing trust in the data, having fewer manual steps in the testing process and showcasing the value proposition of A/B testing.	Running more tests at once now that there is a culture of experimentation within the product engineering organization.	Improving insights gained from each test and shortening time to gain insights on user, product, and business metrics.	Standardizing advanced experimentation techniques so all teams at the company can leverage them.
Key Experimentation Practices Metrics	Number of successfully completed A/B tests.	Percentage of teams adopting A/B testing (e.g., "60% of product teams ran an experiment within the past quarter").	Increase in the number of parallel experiments without compromising quality.	Percentage of experiments that yield actionable insights.	Ability to measure long-term effects with holdbacks (seamlessly).

The beginning stage is always oriented toward increasing testing adoption, especially when product changes were pushed straight to production for all users to engage with before an experimentation platform existed. This early stage also includes deciding whether to build your platform in-house or opt for a third-party solution. Additionally, it's when you begin developing the data infrastructure needed to generate insights from test results to inform product decisions.

In the intermediate stage, you've already been running experiments with a fairly sustainable process and are now ready to focus on more advanced techniques. At this point, the effect of changes to the product on crucial metrics is significant at your company and the demands of A/B testing are increasing, putting your platform in the intermediate stage. The goal of advancing practices beyond the intermediate stage is to:

- Increase the user and product insights you gain from each experiment.

- Decrease the cost of experimenting from a process, time, and energy perspective.

- Improve the rate of experimenting so that more features are evaluated at once without reducing the quality or validity of the test.

During the intermediate stages, pinpointing opportunities for advancing your already operational A/B testing process can be challenging. To make it easier, use the three focus areas—experimentation rate, quality, and cost—as a starting point to brainstorm the areas for improvement. We'll discuss these three focus areas in detail in the following chapters.

Before getting into why experimentation rate, quality, and cost are essential to improving A/B testing practices on a product, let's first introduce a company that needs more effective testing tactics to continue innovating.

Experimenting at MarketMax

MarketMax, our fictitious e-commerce company, provides artists and small businesses with a platform to sell handcrafted and small-batch goods. You were recently hired as an engineer on the experimentation team to help the company evolve its A/B testing practices.

During your onboarding week, you learned that MarketMax is pivoting its product vision to incorporate more machine learning while maintaining the legacy product as teams figure out the new strategy. With this in mind, the company needs to make the A/B testing platform more robust, easier, and less costly to gain the insights the business and product teams require with this new frontier ahead of them. This is exciting because you know a surprisingly large amount of infrastructure and software is required to scale and evolve an A/B test platform, which means your engineering skill set will be well utilized at MarketMax.

The following wireframe illustrates MarketMax's e-commerce website. Take note of the personalized recommendations and algorithmic-driven components. The product team aims to continue to evolve and improve the use of machine learning within the product.

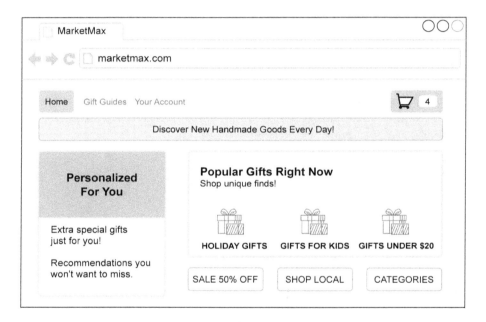

Now that you have a general idea of the product experience, let's see the current state of MarketMax's experimentation practices.

Getting Ready for Experimenting

For years, teams at MarketMax have been conducting experiments to evaluate the effectiveness of their product and engineering strategy. As the company has grown and the product has scaled to millions of users, the A/B testing platform is encountering testing space constraints, quality issues, and process bottlenecks.

Today, the platform can support a good number of experiments; however, the time it takes to configure the test varies—sometimes it's straightforward, but more often than not, too much time is spent coordinating with other teams to ensure the results are valid.

The platform is also constrained from a resourcing perspective; there are more tests that the product team wants to run compared to the number of users to evaluate against. To illustrate precisely where MarketMax is in its experimentation journey, let's jump into your first Engineer Task.

Engineer Task: Pinpoint Where MarketMax Is in Their Experimentation Journey

Given the information you have thus far about MarketMax's experimentation practices, do you think they are at the beginning, intermediate, or advanced level?

 Engineer Task: Where do you think MarketMax stands in terms of their experimentation practices?

MarketMax's experimentation practices wouldn't be considered at the beginning stage, given that the culture of an experimentation-driven product is already set; they're no longer battling whether to run A/B tests but, rather, when and how. If you're thinking they fall within the intermediate stage, then you're exactly right! Although the platform has a self-service application enabling teams to set up experiments, there's a desire to make more improvements to enable better coordination and quicker insights.

You'll help the team improve their A/B testing methods with new techniques by focusing on three key areas: experimentation rate, quality, and cost. Let's start by examining what it takes to improve a product's experimentation rate.

Increasing Experimentation Rate

If you're only able to run one test at a time, the rate at which you're running experiments is low. If the platform supports many tests at once but still blocks some tests from launching, consider solutions that can increase the experimentation rate.

In practice, you need to increase your experimentation rate if the following occurs:

- Experiments are blocked from launching due to insufficient user traffic, limiting the ability to gather statistically significant results.

- Experiments take too long to deliver actionable insights, causing delays in critical product and business decisions.

- Experiments are often paused and restarted later to enable another higher-priority experiment to run on the platform.

Let's see how MarketMax explored ways to improve their platform and practices by focusing on their experimentation rate.

Identifying Experimentation Platform Improvements

At MarketMax, the experimentation team aims to adapt and grow alongside the company's evolving product strategy. Because remember, without the right tactics to evaluate product ideas, how do you really know you're making the metric improvements that you set forth to achieve?

To better understand where improvements can be made in the end-to-end process of experimenting on the product, the team ran a workshop.

This workshop helped diagnose the current situation—what's working well and what needs improvement. To really understand the scope of problems and even frustrations from teams that run A/B tests on the product, the experimentation platform team also surveyed its users before the workshop to have data points ahead of the discussion.

Many questions were asked, including the following:

- How do you ensure an experiment is set up correctly before launching?

- How do you QA the product experience for users allocated into the test and control variants?

- How much time did your team spend configuring each test? How many tests have been blocked from launching because of space issues or engineering constraints?

- How do you do configure an A/B test designed to answer your team's specific use cases on the product?

At the end of the workshop, the team aggregated the answers to these questions and produced a handful of visualizations to identify areas for improvement. For example, see the image shown on page 9 that illustrates the percentage of experiments from the past quarter that did not deviate from the original start and end date, delayed the start date, or extended the end date.

Identifying improvements to an experimentation platform that's already reasonably functional is challenging, which is why the platform team spent time and energy running the workshop and crafting a thoughtful survey. The overarching goal of the workshop is to understand the primary pain points and blockers for A/B testing. Most platform teams are often detached from

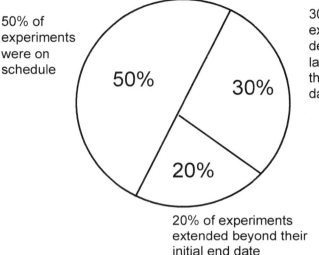

50% of experiments were on schedule

30% of experiments were delayed; launching past the initial start date

20% of experiments extended beyond their initial end date

how their tools are used, so without frequent touchpoints and user feedback, it's hard to gauge what's really working. Meeting with users of the platform to understand their pain points is an excellent practice for any platform team but especially an experimentation platform team because the practice of A/B testing on a product is far different from the theory.

Next, let's analyze the data gathered from the experimentation workshop at MarketMax to identify areas for improvement in the end-to-end testing process.

Facilitating an Experimentation Workshop

Organizing an experimentation workshop is worthwhile only if it provides valuable data as to how teams use the A/B testing platform. To get data, you need to ask users of the platform questions in the form of a survey. How you frame your questions will directly influence the quality of the insights from the answers.

Don't ask quantitative questions like the following at your experimentation workshop: "How many experiments did you run this past quarter?" You can do that analysis up front prior to the workshop or via a survey before the workshop. Instead ask teams, "What is the most valuable outcome you've observed from running an experiment on the product?" Consider using the following list of questions as a starting point for crafting surveys for an experimentation workshop:

1. Do you have the right metrics to measure the impact of a change on the product?

2. What is the hardest step while setting up an experiment on the product?

3. Do you have low confidence in your experiment setup before you launch the experiment to users?

4. Have there been instances when you couldn't start an experiment? If so, what was the reason for delaying the experiment?

5. What is your QA process before starting the experiment?

6. Do you have a clear checklist for ending an experiment?

7. How do you decide which metrics to monitor during an experiment?

8. Is there a step in the experiment setup process that takes longer than expected? What is it, and why?

9. Have you ever had to restart an experiment after launch? If so, what caused the restart?

10. Do you have clear guidelines for deciding when to end an experiment?

11. Are there parts of the experimentation workflow that feel redundant or unnecessary?

12. Is rerunning experiments to double down or revalidate insights a best practice on your team?

These questions are designed to uncover detailed, practical insights about teams' experiences with the experimentation platform, helping you identify pain points and prioritize improvements. Each question ladders up to a key category in the experimentation process. See the diagram shown on page 11, a mind map illustrating topics that you can include in your workshop.

This mind map showcases the categories and subcategories for an experimentation workshop, encompassing critical areas such as prelaunch verification, active monitoring, variant configuration, and experiment outcomes. It serves as a guide to identify pain points for improving experimentation practices.

For instance, the Experiment End subcategory should center on questions related to the key steps, best practices, and challenges involved in effectively concluding an experiment. This includes ensuring accurate data validation, analyzing results, and deciding on next steps based on the findings. It's an opportunity to explore how teams document learnings and make decisions informed by experiment outcomes.

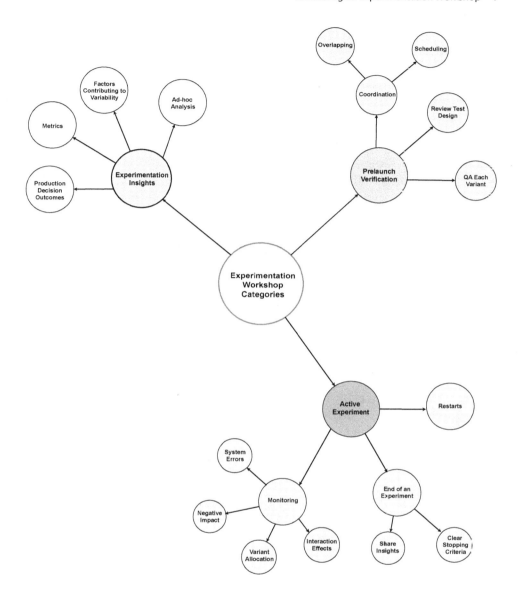

Similarly, the Experimentation Monitoring category should focus on how teams keep an eye on experiments while they're in progress. Key areas to ask questions on include monitoring metrics for anomalies, maintaining data integrity, and managing unexpected issues such as degradations in performance or skewed traffic allocation. This subcategory helps uncover gaps in real-time tracking and identify opportunities for improving experiment health checks.

The Experimentation Coordination subcategory is vital for understanding how engineering and product teams align their efforts when resources are constrained. Questions here should aim to uncover how conflicts are resolved when multiple teams need to run experiments simultaneously but face limited testing capacity. This category can also explore questions that illustrate how teams manage prioritization, communication, and collaboration across teams to ensure experimentation runs smoothly.

Additionally, the Experimentation Restart subcategory addresses an area that is often overlooked: understanding the causes and impacts of restarting experiments. Questions in this category should focus on understanding why experiments are restarted, whether due to misconfigurations, metric inaccuracies, or unforeseen technical issues. It's essential to delve into how these restarts affect timelines, team productivity, and confidence in the experimentation process. This subcategory can also highlight the importance of robust QA processes, clear setup guidelines, and automated validation tools to reduce the likelihood of restarts. By identifying common pain points, this focus area can help drive improvements in experiment reliability and efficiency.

The Factors Contributing to Variability category is important for understanding why experiment results may lack consistency or reliability. Questions in this area should focus on identifying sources of variability, such as seasonality, external events, user behavior changes, or even metric sensitivity. It's important to explore how teams account for variability during experiment design and whether they use techniques such as segmentation or variance reduction to mitigate its impact. This category can also explore how variability affects each team's decision-making framework. Depending on how you scope your questions, you could highlight when it's necessary to run follow-up experiments. By asking questions related to variability in experiment insights, you'll better understand how teams interpret the results of their A/B tests.

Asking good questions is an art; the more effort you invest in drafting your experimentation workshop survey, the better insights you'll glean. A good question leads to informative answers that you can then take action on. To craft a well-formatted question, you should be specific in the phrasing and scope. Effectively use the time you have with the teams that leverage the A/B testing platform by asking good questions.

Now that you have a good idea of what questions to ask at an experimentation workshop, let's tackle your next Engineer Task.

Engineer Task: Analyzing Experimentation Workshop Results

As a new engineer on the experimentation team at MarketMax, you'll help the team interpret the initial insights gathered from the workshop. Specifically, what conclusions can you draw from the data presented in the pie chart on page 9?

 Engineer Task: What conclusions would you draw from the results of the MarketMax experimentation workshop?

To summarize, 50 percent of tests launched on the experimentation platform had the correct configuration and did not require an extension or an early termination. And 50 percent of experiments were either extended or delayed.

What could be the cause for an experiment to continue beyond the predefined end date? In practice, two core reasons account for a test's duration to change: the test needed to run longer to collect enough data for metrics to be sufficiently powered, or the test was delayed and didn't start on the original date.

One reason an experiment gets delayed and is launched after the initial start date is when the current QA process takes too long to validate a test. In these cases, optimizing the verification techniques with new tooling and infrastructure is a good idea.

Another reason why an experiment may have a delayed start date is when there isn't enough testing space that would lend itself to prioritizing more advanced techniques that either require fewer users or share users across multiple experiments.

In cases where experiments require a longer duration to gain more data, you're subsequently blocking new experiments from launching. To address this, the team may need to build techniques that enable teams to run more tests in parallel. These are just a few of the practical strategies that we'll discuss in more detail in Chapter 2, Improving Experimentation Throughput, on page 25.

You might think that starting an experiment late or extending its duration isn't a big deal—teams just wait a bit longer, right? Not quite. Delays in experimentation slow down product innovation. The longer you wait to start a test or get results, the longer your teams go without the data they need to make informed decisions. That's why experimentation rate is a critical characteristic of a mature engineering platform.

In the same way that improving the rate relies on more advanced testing techniques, improving the quality of insights also requires leveling up your A/B testing practices. Let's examine why improving the quality of A/B test results is key to advancing your experimentation platform.

Improving Experimentation Quality

The quality of an experiment directly impacts the decisions you can make to evolve your product. In this context, quality refers to the insights gathered and the validity of the test setup. For example, suppose that tests are often broken or misconfigured. In that case, the experiment quality is low, and you should prioritize building better tooling that can catch issues earlier. While being more diligent during experiment setup is helpful in theory, it's not enough in practice. Teams need robust tooling and systems to validate test configurations and ensure experiment integrity.

You should consider prioritizing experimentation quality if the following occurs:

- Teams are running experiments longer, beyond the predefined end date, to gain more data because the success and guardrail metrics are inefficient for deciding whether to roll out the change.

- Teams are finding that tests are inconclusive, resulting in a lack of insights to inform whether a feature should launch.

- Teams are not consistently evaluating changes in the scope of an experiment because there's more effort required to derive insights and compute metrics.

- Teams are forgoing more complex experiments, such as long-term holdbacks, because the results aren't reliable or trusted.

- Teams are launching more misconfigured experiments or experiments that lack statistical significance.

Improving experimentation quality aims to increase the number of clean, effective tests that make their way to production. To illustrate this, let's look at a visualization from a survey conducted by the MarketMax experimentation team. The survey was sent to teams that ran A/B tests on the platform, and the visualization benchmarks test outcomes at a detailed level. See the image shown on page 15.

The pie chart aggregates the outcome from each experiment that launched on the product into three categories: an experiment that was configured correctly but

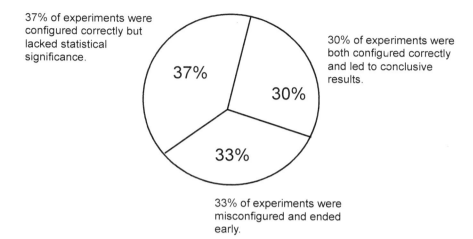

37% of experiments were configured correctly but lacked statistical significance.

30% of experiments were both configured correctly and led to conclusive results.

33% of experiments were misconfigured and ended early.

lacked statistical significance; an experiment that was configured correctly and led to product insights, given the results were conclusive; and an experiment that was misconfigured and ended before its predefined end date.

With these benchmarks, you can more precisely understand what the experimentation platform at MarketMax is doing well and where improvements can be made.

Before we discuss further how to improve experimentation quality, how do you think you should increase the number of clean, correctly configured experiments that launch on the MarketMax product? Check out your next Engineer Task.

Engineer Task: Improving Testing Quality

As you can see from the pie chart, 33 percent of experiments were aborted early because the team noticed unexpected behavior in the user experience as a result of misconfiguration. How do you think the team at MarketMax could improve this statistic?

 Engineer Task: What strategies can improve experimentation quality?

Similarly, 37 percent of the tests were configured correctly; however, they did not yield statistically significant results, providing no actionable product or user insights from the experiment.

The goal of evaluating experimentation quality is not to measure how successfully you build new products that impact users positively but to measure how effective you are at running high-quality tests. With that in mind, what type of strategies would you build to increase the number of high-quality experiments?

You may have considered improving the QA process for validating an experiment configuration before it's in front of users. Creating tooling to enable an easier and standardized QA process is a great tactic that can decrease the chances of launching misconfigured tests to your users.

Implementing variant reduction strategies to better understand the true impact of changes to product and user metrics is another idea. You could also leverage cohorts to understand who the new feature works well for versus who it doesn't. Both user cohorts and variance reduction strategies are one of the many solutions we'll discuss further in Chapter 6, Ensuring Trustworthy Insights, on page 119.

Not all tests have an outcome suggesting the feature should be rolled out to all users. It's important to point this out because you don't want to encourage teams to exclusively run experiments that they are very confident will work, since the potentially riskier tests could have the highest potential for success. Always remember that the goal of measuring experimentation quality is to ensure you learn as much as possible from every online evaluation by configuring high-quality A/B tests.

Next, we'll explore why decreasing the cost of running experiments on your product is critical in advancing your A/B testing practices.

Decreasing Experimentation Cost

The word "cost" when used in the experimentation domain, has two distinct definitions: infrastructure cost and resourcing cost.

Infrastructure cost is the monetary amount allocated to the systems and data pipelines that enable the A/B testing platform and the surrounding systems that the platform relies on. For example, it's the monetary cost of running pipelines and services in your cloud provider, such as AWS or GCP. Resourcing cost refers to the time and energy needed to configure, run, and summarize the results of an A/B test.

In this context, experimentation cost will refer to resourcing cost—the time and energy needed to run experiments on your product. Decreasing experimentation costs should be considered if you find that many teams are involved in configuring an experiment or that many hours are required to ensure the configuration is valid before launching. If numerous experiments are paused or restarted due to misconfiguration issues resulting in a broken user experience, then simplifying the process to validate whether an experiment is correctly set up is a great way to reduce the costs of running experiments on a product.

You want experimentation to be so seamless from a cost perspective that time and energy are never a reason for not running an A/B test. When investments in the experimentation practices on a product are made, the cost of running an experiment reduces and teams can focus more on designing meaningful hypotheses and interpreting results rather than troubleshooting setup issues. Lowering experimentation costs also fosters a culture of innovation, as teams are more likely to test ideas—big or small—without being deterred by resource constraints.

Let's revisit experimenting at MarketMax. To identify areas for improvement, the experimentation team conducted a resourcing cost analysis, evaluating the time and effort spent configuring A/B tests over the past quarter. Take a look at the following scatter plot for your next Engineer Task:

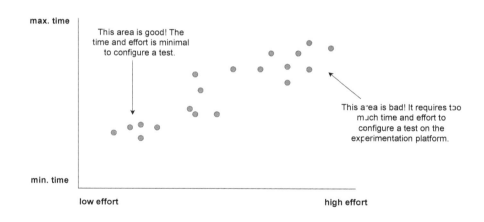

Experiment setup: time and effort cost analysis

Engineer Task: Interpreting Experimentation Cost Analysis

Taking a look at the scatter plot on page 17, how would you interpret the cost analysis comparing time spent and energy exerted when configuring an experiment on MarketMax's experimentation platform? Would you say time spent to configure the test is low? Or would you say setting up a test on the experimentation platform took a fair amount of effort and time?

 Engineer Task: How would you interpret the MarketMax cost analysis?

It's clear that MarketMax runs many experiments; however, the time and effort required to enable these experiments on the product lean toward the more costly spectrum of the chart. The more time teams spend setting up an experiment, the less ideal this evaluation strategy is for urgent or high-priority changes that need to be launched as soon as possible.

When configuring an A/B test requires too much effort, it's easier to miss a key detail, resulting in a broken experiment launching to your users. If the friction to set up an experiment is too high, teams are more likely to get frustrated with the process and, as a result, bypass this critical step of the product development life cycle.

Having easy-to-use tools and clear experimentation guidelines go a long way when scaling your experimentation platform to meet the needs of a company that's already practicing A/B testing changes on a product. You'll be surprised at how effective, clear A/B testing templates can reduce the cost of experimenting for teams seeking to evaluate changes on a product.

The more experiments you run on a product, the more challenges you'll come across. That's the beauty of A/B testing. As a company grows and continues to evolve, A/B testing will need to do the same.

Now that we've detailed why experimentation rate, cost, and quality are important factors, let's consider some guiding principles to keep in mind as you implement strategies to take your experimentations practices to the next level.

Guiding Principles

When practicing experimentation at scale, debates about where to focus improvements are inevitable. The priorities often depend on who you are talking to:

- A data scientist might prioritize methodologies that increase the depth of insights from each experiment.

- An engineer might focus on optimizing the infrastructure and tools that power experimentation across the product.

- A product manager likely values streamlined processes and user-friendly tooling to quickly launch A/B tests with minimal friction.

- A UX designer may emphasize understanding how experiments impact user experience, advocating for metrics and methodologies that capture user behavior and satisfaction.

While these perspectives are all valid, they highlight a critical truth: you can't improve every aspect of experimentation simultaneously. Nor can you implement every framework or strategy you come across—it may not align with your product's needs or industry-specific challenges.

To make meaningful progress, it's important to have a set of guiding principles that help you decide where to focus your efforts. These principles ensure that experimentation evolves in a way that's practical, impactful, and sustainable for your team and organization.

As you explore this book and uncover tactics and methodologies to implement in your work, keep the following principles in mind:

1. Keep complexity and simplicity in balance.
2. Implement for scalability and sustainability.
3. Minimize experimentation obstacles.

The following flowchart shows how these three guiding principles—minimizing obstacles, implementing scalable and sustainable solutions, and balancing complexity with simplicity—are interconnected.

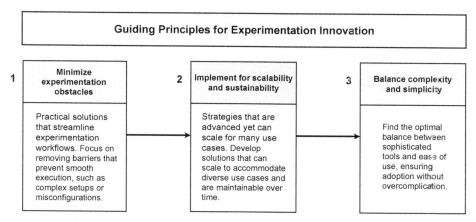

The chart highlights how each principle builds upon and reinforces the others, creating a cohesive framework for driving continuous improvement in experimentation practices. Let's explore each principle in greater detail.

Balancing Complexity and Simplicity

Complex experiments may provide more insight, but they also carry higher risks and require more resources. You need to balance complexity with the ability to draw clear, actionable conclusions. Striking the right balance between complexity and simplicity is critical to ensuring that your strategies are both actionable and widely adopted.

Ask yourself the following:

• Can someone without deep experimentation expertise understand and use this new strategy or framework?

• Is there sufficient tooling, documentation, and support to enable its adoption?

If the answer is no, you might need to invest time in building the necessary infrastructure or reevaluate whether the approach is the right fit. A strategy that looks promising on paper may not be the right fit for your product or engineering ecosystem if it's too complex for widespread use or lacks scalability.

Complexity isn't a bad thing—in fact, it's often necessary for advanced experimentation strategies. With the right engineering architecture, processes, and tools, even the most intricate strategies can be made manageable. The goal isn't to avoid complexity but to make it work for you. Focus on understanding how a strategy works, implementing it thoughtfully, and scaling it so that teams across your organization can use it easily. When done right, experimentation should empower teams to move faster and make better decisions—not slow them down with unnecessary barriers.

Keeping It Sustainable While Scaling

Scalability and sustainability go hand in hand when building experimentation practices. A new methodology might sound appealing, but consider this: if your engineering team struggles to implement or maintain it in production, it won't gain traction or scale effectively.

Start small. Prototype new strategies and test them on a handful of experiments. Use these case studies to understand how the strategy performs in practice—what works, what doesn't, and where adjustments are needed. It's easy to be blinded by well-written research papers that paint the picture of vast improvements to your experimentation rate, cost, and quality and forget how expensive it can be to support or implement at scale. For this reason, try not to jump toward a full, platformized solution. It's best to prototype the new experiment strategy first, develop a handful of practical case studies by using the new experimentation strategy on the product, and then determine if you can scale the strategy so that it can be used by many teams experimenting on the product.

Don't optimize prematurely. Avoid the temptation to prematurely build a full platformized solution. You should live by the iterative, prototyping approach. Only after you've demonstrated success via practical use cases on the product, should you scale the strategy for broader use. This approach minimizes wasted resources and ensures that the solutions you implement are grounded in practicality.

Minimizing Obstacles

One of the biggest barriers to a culture of experimentation is when an obstacle is in the way of a team that eagerly wants to run an A/B test on the product. Whether it's due to complex processes, unclear metrics, or a lack of reliable tooling, obstacles can discourage teams from launching tests. As you refine your experimentation practices, aim to reduce these barriers.

With each new experimentation strategy, your goal should be to reduce the reasons for an experiment not to launch, whether through precise test design, system improvements, or new experimentation methods.

The act of experimenting on a product is a shared experience between teams that run the test itself and teams that support the infrastructure, data, and insights. By minimizing obstacles, you create an environment where experimentation feels accessible and achievable—regardless of a person's role or expertise.

Keeping It Practical While Innovating

These principles—balancing complexity and simplicity, scaling sustainably, and minimizing obstacles—are the foundation of effective experimentation practices. As you read this book, keep these guidelines top of mind. Each strategy and tactic is designed not only to improve your experimentation capabilities but to do so in ways that are practical, scalable, and impactful. While taking your experimentation practices to the next level, you'll encounter two types of people: those who are well versed in the ins and outs of experimentation and those who simply see the experimentation platform as a tool to help move their project forward. Understanding where most of your platform's users fall on this range of expertise is crucial—it shapes the tools, documentation, and strategies you should prioritize. This is why keeping experimentation practices as practical and accessible as possible while innovating is so important—it ensures everyone, regardless of expertise, can engage with and benefit from the process.

Chapter Roundup: Running an Experimentation Workshop

A/B testing de-risks product and engineering decisions. It's a method that enables you to feel comfortable with the changes you're putting in front of users because you have data to understand the effect. Yet, the longer you invest in setting up an experiment or waiting for test outcomes, the more time it will require to innovate and deliver your new product feature to all users. To identify the gaps or opportunities to advance your A/B testing practices on the product, run an experimentation platform workshop.

Use the following exercises to help you craft the workshop, where you'll include experienced and novice users to identify pain points and bottlenecks in the end-to-end testing process.

- *Exercise 1.* Walk through the process to configure a single test. Take note of any manual steps or any steps in which the tool that orchestrates the A/B testing setup fails to meet the needs of the experiment configuration.

- *Exercise 2.* Observe how users of the experimentation platform QA a test before it's launched on the product. How do they validate whether the test treatment is configured correctly compared to the control? Are there better criteria for evaluating whether a test has been exhaustively QA'ed based on what you observed?

- *Exercise 3.* Run through the process to verify that a test is running correctly after its launch. Is there enough observability in place, such as graphs or dashboards, that would enable a test owner to catch a misconfiguration earlier in the test duration rather than later? Can issues be flagged well before the test has concluded?

- *Exercise 4.* Run through the process to gather data to derive the test results. Are there multiple tools used, or is there standardization for data gathering? Are there many manual steps, or is the process to perform metrics computation programmatically?

By running an A/B testing workshop, you'll be able to gather information about the current process and narrow in on each step to better understand if rate, cost, or quality should be an area of focus for your experimentation platform.

Wrapping Up

Improving experimentation rate, cost, and quality isn't just a nice-to-have—it's foundational to advancing any A/B testing platform. When you invest in your experimentation practices, you're directly influencing the speed and quality of decisions made on a product. A strong A/B testing strategy enables teams to ship and evaluate new features more effectively, leading to better product outcomes.

Let's recap what you've learned in this chapter:

- Running a workshop to observe and survey how users are configuring experiments on the platform to understand where advancements in the experimentation process need to be made.

- Examining how much time and energy is spent configuring and validating a test to determine if the cost of experimentation is an area for improvement.

- Creating benchmarks based on the number of successful, misconfigured, and aborted experiments to pinpoint where experimentation quality can be improved.

- Understanding that many advanced strategies become manageable when paired with the right system architecture, intuitive tools, and well-designed processes. Keep in mind the three guiding principles to ensure that your experimentation evolves in a way that is practical, impactful, and sustainable.

- Facilitating an experimentation workshop and crafting well-defined questions to better understand challenges and obstacles for running A/B tests in the product.

Just as your product evolves to meet your customers' needs, your experimentation platform needs to evolve to keep up with innovation rate, company growth, and improving product insights. We'll explore how to increase testing rate by running more experiments, in parallel, on a product in the next chapter.

CHAPTER 2

Improving Experimentation Throughput

The definition of a successful experimentation strategy at any company is contextual. If you're just getting started with experimentation, running a handful of tests a quarter and gaining user insights from those experiments is great! On the other hand, if you've been practicing A/B testing for years and the demand for experimentation at the company has grown since the initial days of building the platform, running only a handful of tests a quarter is insufficient.

At a certain point, when the demand for A/B testing grows, you'll need to run more tests at once. The success of an experimentation platform hinges on the ability to run as many tests as your product and engineering teams desire while still maintaining validity in the results. If there are bottlenecks, such as not enough users to evaluate against or difficulty understanding how much space you have available to run an experiment, kicking off an experiment is more challenging. Improving the rate at which you can run experiments on your product is essential to continually and reliably utilizing the A/B testing methodology to evaluate changes on a product.

In the previous chapter, you examined the three pillars—rate, quality, and cost—to advance your experimentation practices. In this chapter, we'll be looking further into experimentation rate so you can run more tests at once.

More specifically, you'll explore the following:

- Evaluating different testing strategies to identify their advantages, disadvantages, and appropriate use cases.

- Identifying and addressing pain points related to limited testing space and coordination challenges.

- Implementing tactics to increase experimentation rate and enable more simultaneous tests without compromising validity.

Let's start by looking at what it means to have testing constraints that block experiments from launching.

Reasoning with Limited Testing Availability

Everything has its limits. Your computer only has so much storage before it's maxed out. The oven in your kitchen can only heat to a certain temperature before it stops getting hotter. Experimentation is no different—at some point, the demand for running tests will outgrow what your current strategy can support. Maybe you only have a limited number of users who fit the experiment's targeting criteria or just a few weeks before Marketing rolls out their campaign for a new feature that hasn't been fully tested yet. And here's the tricky part: you can't just "test the important stuff," because what's considered important varies depending on who you ask. A feature that's mission-critical for one team might seem trivial to another, even if both are aligned with the same overarching product goals.

When more teams want to run experiments at the same time, testing space can quickly become scarce. This leads to conflicts, delayed insights, and a lot of frustration. Limited capacity can also stifle innovation—smaller, exploratory tests often get pushed aside in favor of bigger, high-stakes experiments. The result? Great ideas might never make it to the surface.

The good news is there's a way out of this bottleneck. By evolving your experimentation practices and introducing more advanced strategies, you can unlock the ability to run more tests in parallel so teams don't have to fight for testing space.

Let's revisit experimentation at MarketMax to see how testing coordination challenges play out in practice.

Coordinating Tests at MarketMax

MarketMax is a company that truly leverages experimentation. Teams prioritize the experimentation step to better understand the effect of changes on product, business, engineering, and user metrics. Running more online controlled experiments is especially important given that MarketMax is investing more resources into machine learning to improve engagement on the website.

As the product evolves and the company grows, the engineering team is seeing a significant increase in demand for running experiments. Another reason for the increasing demand is that MarketMax is investing more resources into machine learning to improve engagement on the website, which relies heavily on A/B testing. This increase in demand is a positive sign—it's good to have a high-demand experimentation platform. However, it also means it's time to rethink and evolve your strategies to keep pace with this growing demand.

The following image illustrates MarketMax's testing schedule that the experimentation platform supports.

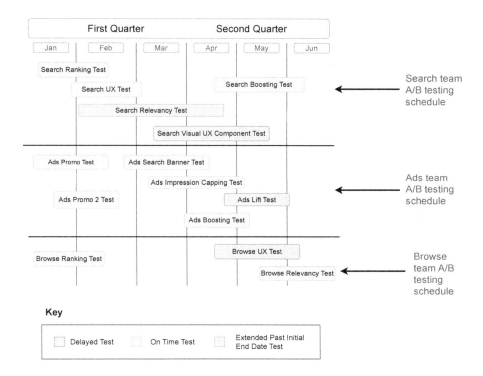

Currently, the experimentation platform primarily works best for configuring isolated experiments, meaning users are only allocated to one experiment at a time. This approach limits the platform's capacity since each user can only be exposed to one variant at any given time. The team wants to implement a strategy where users can be allocated to multiple experiments to increase capacity for running more tests on the product at a given time.

Before figuring out how to increase testing capacity at MarketMax, let's examine a particular delayed test for the Search team in the following Engineer Task.

Engineer Task: Reasoning with Testing Delay

Examining the experiments the Search team executed in the first and second quarters, why do you think the Search Relevancy Test had a delayed start date? Is there a reason that you can gather by looking at the other tests that ran around that time frame that could have caused this particular search test to be delayed?

 Engineer Task: What factors can cause a testing delay?

If you suspected the delay was caused by a shortage of users to run a new experiment while a handful of Search, Ads, and Browse tests were already active, then you're spot on.

Also, did you notice the timing of the Search Relevancy Test? It was planned for the last month of the first quarter, a period of high traffic for most experimentation platforms. You'll often see a bottleneck around the end of each quarter because product and engineering teams aim to meet their quarterly goals.

In practice, when teams face limited testing capacity, they often look for experiments nearing completion, peek at the data to check for significance, and then decide whether to end the test early to free up space. But ending experiments prematurely is just a Band-Aid solution—the real fix is to diagnose and address the root cause of the capacity constraint.

To identify the root cause, you need to understand how teams are designing their experiments in practice.

For example, teams may be running longer tests without well-justified hypotheses or objectives. A good hypothesis should clearly connect product changes to user behavior, outlining how those changes may impact users and their choices. If the experiment lacks a clear hypothesis, it harms your ability to identify and bring value to users and ultimately results in wasted testing space.

Or perhaps teams are running experiments with very large sample sizes. Why would they do this? Simple—they're just following what they think is right, rather than thoughtfully considering what the test actually requires in terms of metric power and minimum detectable effect. Without that reflection, they may be over-investing time and users into experiments that could have been smaller, faster, and equally reliable.

There are also situations where larger sample sizes are necessary—such as multivariate experiments with many variants, or tests with limited exposure to new features in specific areas of the product.

It's important to call out that not all tests are good tests—some are simply flawed from the start. A bad test might have unreasonable statistical power requirements, or it might evaluate changes that don't warrant online, user-facing experimentation in the first place. That's why a clear, well-formed hypothesis is essential: it helps ensure the test is grounded in meaningful product and engineering context and that the decision to evaluate the change online makes sense.

Let's look at the most common signs that suggest testing availability and coordination are a problem on an experimentation platform.

Visualizing Testing Availability

You're likely to encounter testing coordination challenges in several situations. If your testing strategy restricts users from entering multiple experiments at a given time, it inherently limits the number of experiments your platform can support. While isolated experiments have their benefits, they also constrain your testing capacity. Additionally, long test durations prevent users from being deallocated and reassigned to new experiment treatments, further complicating the coordination of experiments.

If you tentatively plan an experiment to launch next week, how do you know if you have enough availability on the platform to run the experiment? Or if you're aiming to run an isolated experiment, how do you know if the users you're targeting aren't already allocated to another experiment? When testing space capacity is difficult to grok, it will be even harder to forecast and plan your product roadmap that relies on the results of an experiment to make product decisions.

Tooling is key to demystifying how much space is available. In fact, effective tooling is foundational to all experimentation best practices, especially as your platform evolves to support a higher volume of concurrent experiments. You'll see that tooling is a recurring theme throughout this book. As experimentation strategies become more advanced, effective tools become critical for managing the added complexity and enabling teams to adopt the new tactic for evaluating features on a product.

Building a simple user interface (UI) in your experimentation platform can make it easier to see how much capacity is available to run new experiments. With a proper UI, anyone at the company should be able to determine how much testing capacity is available at a given time, forecast when to run a test so other teams can view and anticipate adjusting their plans if space constraints exist, and anticipate coordination issues so teams can adjust the product roadmap and experimentation plans ahead of time.

The following image is an example of a visualization representing the testing capacity on the experimentation platform.

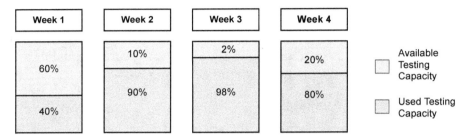

Relying on a manual process to coordinate tests and forecast testing space can make your experimentation workflow fragile and error prone. When teams are calculating availability by hand, missteps are more likely—and costly. By building tooling that automatically computes testing availability, you reduce friction and make it easier for anyone in the company to understand current constraints and plan their next experiment with confidence.

Another visualization that's helpful to illustrate a team's testing capacity is a timeline representation of current and upcoming tests with sample size annotations (in brackets) and testing availability computed by the experimentation platform. Simple tools can have a profound effect on your experimentation process. See the following image.

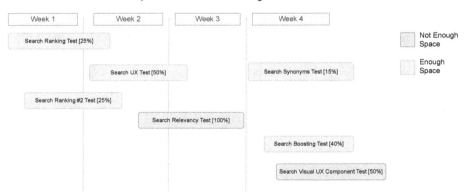

Think of this timeline like your work calendar when scheduling meetings. If you accidentally book three meetings at the same time—or, more realistically, get scheduled into three meetings despite your clearly marked Focus

Time—you're obviously overbooked and need to shuffle things around. The same principle applies to experiments on a product. If three experiments are planned to run simultaneously and there's a testing limitation, you'll need to coordinate and reschedule to avoid a bottleneck. Just like meetings, sometimes it's less about the availability and more about managing the chaos with tooling.

With the right tooling to visualize testing availability, you can spot traffic jams early instead of scrambling at the last minute to unblock a team from running their experiment.

It's also important to consider how teams use this tooling. Even with seamless tools, a strong process is necessary in the experimentation domain. Ideally, teams would create placeholders for the dates they plan to launch experiments. If teams don't forecast their testing timelines, it becomes much harder to plan ahead, and you may still face last-minute adjustments.

Now that we've discussed what limited space looks like in practice and how to visualize your testing capacity, let's explore the different testing strategies.

Varying Testing Strategies

The overall theme of this chapter is to enable more tests to run simultaneously, increasing experimentation throughput on a product. The less waiting and schedule wrangling needed, the better the experience your product and engineering teams will have as they utilize the platform to evaluate changes to the product.

These are most common testing strategies:

1. Sequential testing
2. Multivariate testing
3. Isolated testing
4. Overlapping testing

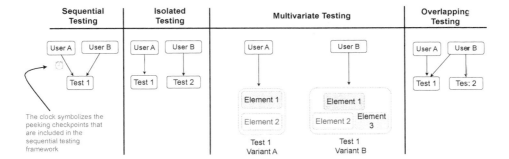

Each strategy differs in its approach. For example, sequential testing has peeking checkpoints where analysis occurs at different stages, while the isolated testing strategy doesn't include checkpoints and analysis is performed only after all data has been collected at the end of an experiment.

While all four strategies can be useful, it's important to know when to use each one based on the specific use case. It's helpful to have all four testing strategies as tools in your experimentation tool kit, given that product use cases and feature evaluations differ depending on the intent of the experiment and what the team aims to learn.

Regardless of the testing strategy you choose, it's crucial to consult with experienced data scientists who have historical knowledge of how new features and key metrics have interacted in the past. This knowledge will help influence the ideal testing strategy for your use case.

Let's take a closer look at each testing strategy in more detail in the following sections.

Peeking and Ending Tests Early with Sequential Testing

The first strategy we'll explore is the sequential testing paradigm. Unlike the traditional fixed-horizon or fixed-size test, sequential testing does not require committing to a fixed sample size for the control and test variants. Instead, sequential testing allows for continuous monitoring of test results, a process known as *peeking*, where you can check results at various checkpoints during the experiment and stop the test early if significant results are detected.

See the following image to compare the traditional fixed-horizon experiment design versus the sequential experiment.

	Sequential Testing	Fixed Size Testing
Is the sample size set in advance?	No	Yes
Can you peek at the data?	Yes	No
Can you end the test early?	Yes	No

With sequential testing, you have the flexibility to analyze data as it's collected while the experiment is still active. This allows for interim analyses, where statistical checks are performed to avoid false interpretations and maintain the integrity of the results.

You'll find several advantages to peeking at your test early by running a sequential test. First, you can end an experiment early if it's degrading key metrics to reduce the metric hit on a longer timeline. Second, you can end an experiment early if it's performing well from a metrics standpoint by launching the change to all users to continue to affect metrics positively but at a larger scale. Third, you can use the platform's testing resources more efficiently by reducing the time and sample size.

On the other hand, you'll also find several disadvantages to running a sequential test. First, the novelty effect, when a new feature is introduced to users and engagement increases but then fades after the initial exposure, may be harder to detect if you end an experiment early because the insights look promising. Second, looking at test results early could lead to premature decisions, potentially favoring a version of the new feature that appears successful initially but doesn't perform well over time.

The sequential testing strategy can improve your experiment rate by allowing you to end tests early based on interim results, unlike traditional fixed-horizon experiments. For example, if you observe positive gains in your success metrics and stop a test early, you can quickly start another experiment with the freed-up users. This approach is especially beneficial for experiments focused on revenue or other business metrics, as launching a feature that boosts revenue sooner is economically advantageous. You naturally want to launch a feature that increases revenue sooner rather than later from an economic standpoint.

Sequential testing has multiple subtypes, such as group sequential testing and always-valid inference. For more details on these two types of sequential testing, consider reading the following papers: "Group Sequential Designs: A Tutorial"[1] and "Anytime-Valid Linear Models and Regression Adjusted Causal Inference in Randomized Experiments."[2]

Now that you're familiar with sequential testing, let's define the multivariate testing strategy.

---

1. https://psyarxiv.com/x4azm/
2. https://arxiv.org/abs/2210.08589

Evaluating More with Multivariate Tests

Multivariate testing involves presenting more than one change to users within a test variant. A multivariate experiment typically includes several test variants, each evaluating different combinations of these changes to identify the most effective configuration. It's particularly useful for optimizing complex designs, as it allows you to test combinations in a single experiment rather than running separate tests for each change.

The advantages of multivariate testing include its ability to provide holistic design insights by showing how changes work together rather than in isolation. It also improves efficiency by combining several changes into one experiment, saving time and resources, compared to running multiple separate tests. However, there are some drawbacks to consider. Multivariate testing typically requires larger sample sizes and longer durations to achieve statistically significant results, given the factorial nature of the test. Additionally, the analysis can be complex, as it's often challenging to isolate which specific change drives observed outcomes, especially when interactions between variables come into play.

One of the key themes throughout this book is the importance of having a clear hypothesis, no matter which strategy you use to evaluate changes in an online controlled setting. This principle is especially relevant to multivariate testing. To implement multivariate testing effectively, it's crucial to start with a well-defined hypothesis that outlines the experiment's goals and expected outcomes. A clear hypothesis keeps the test focused and actionable, ensuring it aligns with your product or design objectives while helping you navigate the unique benefits and challenges of this approach.

If your goal is to understand a combination of changes that ladder to a holistic product vision with less concern about attributing metric effects to specific features, multivariate testing is an excellent strategy to use. However, if your goal is to understand the specific impact of a particular feature, strategies like isolated or sequential testing may be more effective than multivariate testing. A key theme throughout this book is the importance of clearly understanding the intent of your experiment. If you're not sure what impact you're trying to measure, you're more likely to choose the wrong strategy for evaluating the change on a subset of users.

Now that we've covered multivariate testing, let's dive deeper into isolated testing in the following section.

Assessing the Isolated Testing Strategy

In the isolated testing strategy, users are allocated to only one experiment variant at a time. Multiple experiments can be running simultaneously, but a user will only be assigned to a new test after they have been deallocated from the current test or once the test has ended.

To illustrate, see the following image. Users from Segment A can be allocated to Experiment 3 because it starts after Experiment 1 ends. However, users from Segment B cannot be assigned to Experiment 3, because Experiment 2 is active when Experiment 3 starts.

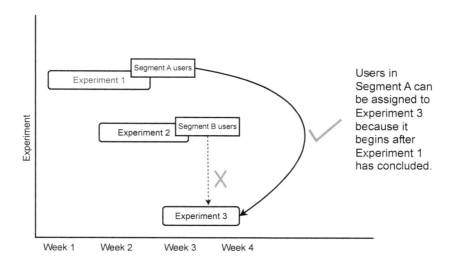

The isolated testing approach gives you two advantages: a higher likelihood that you'll measure true effect because users are exposed to one new feature or change on the product at a time and an increase of precision in measuring the impact of a change on critical metrics.

As for the pitfalls of isolated testing, consider the following: your testing capacity is clearly reduced because users can only be assigned to one experiment at time. Teams are blocked from launching new experiments as they wait for current experiments to conclude to free up users that can then be assigned to a new experiment. In practice, teams will have to wait for an experiment to finish to free up users for the next test, creating a bottleneck in their roadmap and product-planning cycles. Consequently, teams may end an experiment prematurely to unblock a new experiment from launching because the limit was reached.

To further illustrate isolated testing, let's revisit experimenting at MarketMax by checking out your next Engineer Task.

Engineer Task: Benefitting from the Isolated Testing Strategy

Can you think of examples where it would be beneficial to use the isolated testing strategy at MarketMax? To help identify suitable use cases, refer to the teams shown in the scheduling visual on page 27.

 Engineer Task: What types of changes will benefit from an isolated experiment?

Search, Ads, and Browse teams all use A/B testing to evaluate their features on the MarketMax website, but their use cases and goals differ. The Browse team typically runs experiments to improve product discovery. The Search team focuses on optimizing the search algorithm, experimenting with ways to improve relevance and the quality of search results, aiming to help users find desired products faster.

The Ads team, however, has a unique focus: understanding the precise impact of changes to ad placement and content on revenue. For the Ads team, it's crucial to accurately quantify the tradeoff between displaying ads and maintaining the user experience. This is especially important at MarketMax where advertisements are critical to the growth of the business. Isolated testing allows a more precise measurement of a feature's impact without interference from other ongoing experiments. For the Ads team, this can be especially important. First, introducing a bad advertisement to the user may negatively impact the user's sentiment toward the MarketMax product offering. If too many served Ads are irrelevant to the user's taste or prior purchase history, the user may be less likely to use the product. Ads can be somewhat of a polarizing experience when not relevant to a user.

Second, introducing an advertisement tied to monetization requires proper attribution. To accurately forecast the impact of a new ad algorithm on sales, a precise evaluation methodology is essential. Isolated experiments ensure that the Ads team's results aren't confounded—meaning influenced or distorted—by other experiments.

Next, let's examine our final testing strategy. This approach enables user allocation to more than one experiment at once, which is the opposite of the isolated testing strategy.

Increasing Testing Space with the Overlapping Testing Strategy

The overlapping test allows users to be assigned to multiple experiments simultaneously.

Choosing the overlapping testing strategy has its advantages from an experimentation rate perspective. You can run more tests at the same time, avoiding delays caused by waiting for more users to become available. Since overlapping tests allow for concurrent experimentation, teams can test changes on the product at once, accelerating the learning process and enabling faster iterations and product improvements.

Despite its benefits, the overlapping testing strategy comes with its own set of challenges that must be carefully managed. One significant disadvantage is the potential for interaction effects, where users' exposure to multiple changes simultaneously can lead to unforeseen outcomes. For example, a positive change in one experiment might be overshadowed by a negative experience in another, making it difficult to disentangle the true impact of each experiment.

Teams must also be well-informed about which types of experiments should or should not overlap. Certain experiments, especially those targeting the same part of the user journey or measuring similar metrics, are more prone to interference and should ideally be isolated. Understanding the nuances of when to opt for overlapping tests versus other strategies requires a deep domain knowledge of both the product and the testing methodology. This is why it's crucial to uplevel the expertise of product and engineering teams, helping them identify the most suitable strategy for each use case.

When to Opt for the Overlapping Testing Strategy

Overlapping tests are not a one-size-fits-all solution. If precision is crucial and isolating changes from other experiments is necessary to achieve more accurate results, overlapping strategies may not be the best choice. For example, experiments that measure the impact of a critical feature launch or high-stakes product change should often avoid overlapping with unrelated tests to ensure clean data and clear insights.

The decision to use overlapping testing should always be guided by the goal of the experiment. Is the purpose of the test to generate broad insights quickly, or is it to rigorously validate a specific hypothesis? Understanding the desired outcome is essential to selecting the most effective testing strategy. Overlapping testing works well when speed and experimentation rate are prioritized, but it may need to be complemented by other strategies for scenarios requiring high precision or minimal interference.

In general, the overlapping testing strategy requires thoughtful implementation, coordination, and ongoing refinement. Keep this top of mind as you introduce overlapping experiments, especially on a product where teams aren't as aware of what other teams are launching or aren't as a familiar with experimentation concepts such as interaction effect.

Let's explore an implementation of the overlapping testing strategy by revisiting experimentation at MarketMax.

Running Overlapping Tests at MarketMax

At MarketMax, historically, the platform has supported isolated tests. As an engineer on the experimentation platform team, you've realized the demand for experimenting on the product is quickly growing, creating a testing traffic jam. Teams are waiting for space to open up to run their experiments.

To increase the volume of tests and, as a result, the experimentation rate, you propose that the team adopt the overlapping testing strategy.

Google addresses the need for overlapping experiments and offers a solution for safely running them in its paper, "Overlapping Experiment Infrastructure: More, Better, Faster Experimentation."[3] Like MarketMax, Google faced testing space constraints—without overlapping tests, the number of experiments that can run simultaneously becomes limited, slowing down the pace of innovation.

As inspiration, you adopt a strategy similar to Google by building a multifactorial system where each factor corresponds to a changeable parameter in the system design that enables the MarketMax product. In practice, a user would be in N experiments simultaneously, where N equals the number of parameters within a layer. It's worth noting that parameters within a "layer" are not independent and should be controlled together, and parameters across layers should be able to act independently.

The parameters for the MarketMax website fall into three categories very similar to layers illustrated in Google's research paper: UX, Search, Ads, and Browse. The image shown on page 39 illustrates these parameters.

---

3.   https://static.googleusercontent.com/media/research.google.com/en//pubs/archive/36500.pdf

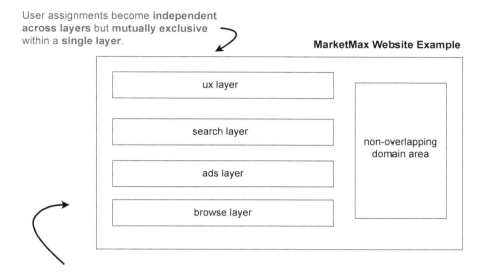

User assignments become **independent across layers** but **mutually exclusive** within a **single layer**.

MarketMax Website Example

ux layer

search layer

ads layer

browse layer

non-overlapping domain area

For example, a single user can participate in up to four experiments at the same time, provided that each experiment modifies settings or configurations within a different layer. However, this is only possible if the user is not already assigned to a non-overlapping experiment, which would prevent their participation in additional tests.

To enable this strategy, the team creates a new concept called "layers" that can be associated with an experiment. Consider the following experiments as an example:

1. Experiment A is tagged with the UX layer.
2. Experiment B is also tagged with the UX layer.
3. Experiment C is tagged with the Search layer.

With these new layer tags associated with experiments, user assignments would be independent for all experiments within the layer. For example, User 1 can be assigned to Experiment A and Experiment C because those two tests can overlap. However, User 1 cannot be in Experiment A or B simultaneously as those two tests cannot overlap, because both tests evaluate changes to the UX layer. See the image shown on page 40.

To enable more tests to run at once, resulting in an increase in experimentation rate, you can use these layer tags to run overlapping tests. For further illustration to architect the overlapping testing strategy, consider reading Google's research paper in depth, as it does a great job of walking through defining the basic overlapping setup. If you're interested in exploring the

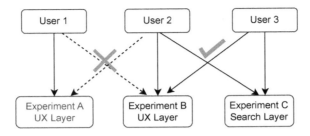

nuances of this approach, Google's paper provides in-depth diagrams and scenarios that greatly influenced MarketMax's implementation.

Creating Best Practices for Overlapping Testing

To maximize the benefits and combat the challenges of the overlapping testing strategy, consider the following best practices:

1. Define clear boundaries.
2. Monitor metrics holistically.
3. Educate teams.
4. Iterate and adjust.

To create a set of best practices to support successful overlapping tests on the product, start by creating clear boundaries by splitting the product areas that experiments target to reduce the risk of interaction effects. You can use heatmaps or user journey maps to identify high-traffic areas and determine where experiments are likely to interact.

Additionally, it's important to monitor metrics holistically to detect subtle interaction effects that may go unnoticed if focusing solely on individual experiments. You can use dashboards that track both individual experiment metrics and aggregate product metrics to identify potential conflicts or unexpected trends.

Similar to any new experimentation strategy, it's critical to educate teams that use the experimentation platform. You should provide product and engineering teams the right amount of knowledge and tools to understand the trade-offs of overlapping testing so that the decision to leverage an over-lapping test versus an isolated test is self-service.

Finally, don't forget to learn from past overlapping experiments to keep improving your approach. Take the time to document what worked well and what didn't—this way, you're building a go-to knowledge base for future decisions. For example, if you notice that overlapping tests targeting similar product features often show interaction effects, it's a sign you might need to rethink your boundaries to influence which changes should be tested in isolation.

By creating best practices, teams can maximize the benefits of overlapping testing while addressing its challenges head-on. When done well, overlapping testing becomes a powerful tool for increasing the rate of experimentation on a product where testing capacity is a concern.

Shifting Experimentation Mindset

Part of advancing your experimentation practices includes evolving how teams think about what an experiment is. Once you have overlapping tests enabled on your platform, it doesn't necessarily mean that teams should evaluate every single idea they have.

To fully embrace these different testing strategies, product and engineering teams must prioritize understanding the experiment's goal. Conducting an experiment that lacks coherence with the product's objectives can be detrimental. It consumes time and engineering resources and may negatively impact the user experience.

It's imperative to articulate the hypothesis clearly and whether your goal is to learn more about a new feature or launch it. Not all experiments lend themselves to supporting both these cases, so it's essential to consider which type of testing strategy your experiment would benefit from while also considering trade-offs, such as space availability, when coordinating a new experiment into the schedule. Although this point has been repeated throughout the chapter, it bears repeating because it's often overlooked when teams rush to meet deadlines, push experiments out the door, and check off weekly status updates. Being intentional about how you design your experiments is key—especially as you start using more advanced strategies. Think carefully about the metrics you're using to measure the impact and the hypothesis you're trying to prove. It's easy to overlook these details, but getting them right can make all the difference in running experiments that actually have an impact on product decisions.

Next let's discuss an important concept that's a main factor in deciding which type of strategy to opt for.

Illustrating Interaction Effects

Let's say you're testing out different pasta recipes. Your first recipe includes pasta, salt, and homemade pesto sauce. Your second recipe includes pasta, salt, and a spicy marinara sauce from your local grocery store. When you taste the first recipe, you think it's great. The fresh pesto sauce adds the right amount of rich flavor. Similarly, when you taste test the second recipe, the spicy sauce has just the right amount of zing. What would it taste like if you combined recipe 1 and recipe 2? They both have salt and pasta, so there are no concerns with these two ingredients. However, the two sauces together are inedible and less tasty than the sauces themselves. In A/B testing, this is similar to an interaction effect.

An interaction effect occurs when a user is exposed to multiple experiments, and the combination of the experiments modifies user engagement in an unanticipated or adverse way compared to observing the results for each experiment independently.

Whether you're comfortable with the possibility of an interaction effect occurring depends on your product and the changes being evaluated. Like the pasta analogy, mixing pesto and spicy marinara may result in an unpleasant interaction effect. However, let's say the first recipe replaced pesto sauce with a good amount of parmesan cheese. In this case, introducing a spicy marinara sauce on top of the first recipe could be really tasty!

In A/B testing, similar positive interaction effects can occur. For example, a product experiment that introduces a new recommendation algorithm might pair well with another experiment that improves the user interface for displaying recommendations. Together, these changes could increase user engagement more than either experiment alone. The key is understanding how the experiments interact with one another—whether they conflict or align.

Managing interaction effects is essential, especially when running overlapping experiments. Some products, like social media platforms or e-commerce websites, have highly interconnected features, making interaction effects more likely. For instance, a change to the checkout process could inadvertently clash with an experiment that modifies pricing display, leading to confusion or frustration for users.

To further illustrate adverse interaction effects, let's return to experimenting at MarketMax.

At MarketMax, many teams are vying to run experiments on the website. In particular, the Search team is aiming to optimize the Search page to return relevant crafts, given a user's recent purchase history and search query terms. Take a look at the following image to visualize what it looks like to have users exposed to multiple experiments, as if the overlapping testing strategy were in use.

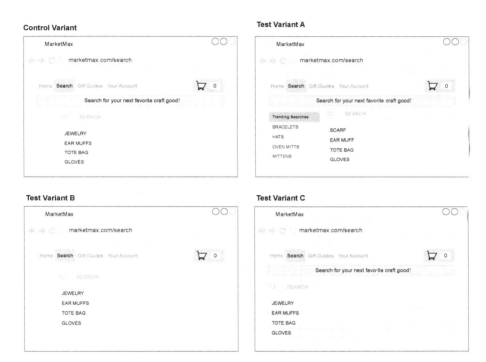

What are the obvious interaction effects for users allocated to test variant A and test variant B? Which variant combinations do you think will result in a bad interaction effect that could lead to a degradation in the user experience?

To answer these questions, start by looking closely at what's changing in each test variant compared to the control.

- Variant A added a Trending Searches component to the left of the search results.

- Variant B removed the "Search for your next favorite craft" header, shifting the search bar and results higher up the page.

- Variant C widened the header, search bar, and results components to take up more space on the website.

Now imagine a user being exposed to variants A and C at the same time. The Trending Searches component (from variant A) could conflict with the widened layout (from variant C), breaking the page and creating a messy, confusing experience. See the following image to visualize how these overlapping changes could clash and lead to a degraded user experience.

Experiences for users exposed to test variants A and C

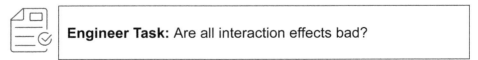

Let's examine these three variants in comparison to the control by checking out your next Engineer Task.

Engineer Task: Interpreting Interaction Effects

Considering the three test variants illustrated on page 43, do you think there's a combination of experiments that would lend itself to an okay overall experience if the same users were allocated into multiple tests via the overlapping testing strategy?

Engineer Task: Are all interaction effects bad?

For instance, if users were exposed to the experiments that evaluated variant A and variant B, the interaction effect would likely be minimal or not harmful to the user experiment. In variant B, the banner above the search bar is removed and in variant A, the trending searches component is added. This, at a glance, seems like an okay combination of changes to be exposed to in a single visit to the MarketMax site. Assigning users to both experiments because of the overlapping test strategy would likely not harm the user experience.

Now suppose the Search team eventually decides to launch both changes illustrated in variants A and B. In that case, you'll naturally run into the interaction effect, which is a benefit to embracing the overlapping testing strategy. If you're thoughtful about deciding which experiments lend themselves to overlaps, you'll actually get a realistic measurement of the impact of the change, as it will likely be alongside other changes (that don't break the user experience, that is).

If you want to run more experiments at the same time and not be constrained by the number of users not already allocated to an experiment, understanding interaction effects is key to deciding when to opt for an overlapping test versus an isolated test.

Now that you're familiar with interaction effects and the different testing strategies, let's consider a few easy-to-follow guidelines.

Defining General Guidelines to Increase Testing Space

Imagine you have a craving for something sweet every morning. Instead of purchasing baked goods, you opt to bake at home. As you collect recipes to try, you realize they all share common steps, like using room-temperature butter and sifting flour. Running an A/B test on a product is similar; every team should adhere to straightforward guidelines to ensure experiments are trustworthy.

Maximizing your testing space efficiently is another strategy that doesn't involve software changes that can impact capacity. To achieve this, establish clear guidelines outlining actions teams can take to conserve space. Just as you always put butter out before baking, teams will develop a habit of consistently following these rules to optimize testing capacity. For instance, if an active test becomes invalid due to misconfiguration or production issues, terminate the test immediately. This ensures users can be reallocated to new experiments instead of continuing with a flawed test.

Similarly, for machine learning evaluations, it's essential to maximize insights before running an online experiment. This can be achieved by requiring teams to thoroughly evaluate their models in an offline setting prior to launching their A/B test. Offline evaluations serve as a critical step in understanding model performance in a controlled environment, allowing teams to refine and optimize their approaches early in the process. By doing so, teams can make more informed decisions and use the online testing space more judiciously, ensuring that only the most promising model variants proceed to A/B testing. One of the significant advantages of offline evaluations is their ability to filter out underperforming model variants. This step not only saves valuable online testing bandwidth but also focuses resources on testing high-potential candidates. Incorporating offline evaluations as a standard practice helps ensure that only well-vetted models are tested in live environments, reducing the risk of wasted effort and improving overall experiment outcomes. We'll discuss offline evaluations in more detail in Chapter 4, Improving Machine Learning Evaluation Practices, on page 75.

Guidelines can also include standards that need to be met for the test to be active. For example, suppose degradations in high-level guardrail metrics, such as app crashes or revenue, pass a certain threshold. In that case, the test should stop and users can be deallocated from the experiment. Once the users are deallocated, they can be reassigned to a new experiment. There's no value in running an experiment that won't launch because of the severity of metric degradation. More often than not, a degradation to a key metric, like browser crashes, results from a code defect or test misconfigurations, which is an excellent reason to stop an experiment and revisit once the issue is resolved.

There should also be monitoring systems in place that automatically alert teams when one of these standards has not been met, enabling swift action to abort the test without requiring manual verification. This type of proactive monitoring ensures that issues such as skewed traffic allocation, metric anomalies, or technical misconfigurations are caught early, minimizing their impact on both users and the experiment's validity. By automating these alerts, teams can respond quickly to prevent poor user experiences from persisting and ensure that data integrity is maintained.

Automated monitoring and early intervention are particularly crucial in high-scale environments where dozens or even hundreds of experiments may be running simultaneously. Without these safeguards, issues in individual tests can go unnoticed, consuming valuable resources and introducing noise into aggregated metrics. A robust monitoring framework supports better outcomes for individual experiments and strengthens the reliability of the entire experimentation practice on a product.

No matter which testing strategy you choose, establishing clear experimentation standards and guidelines helps ensure you're making the best use of time and platform resources by avoiding poorly designed or ineffective online evaluations. To determine the most suitable testing strategy for evaluating a specific feature, you can use the decision tree below as a helpful guide.

Testing Strategy Decision Tree

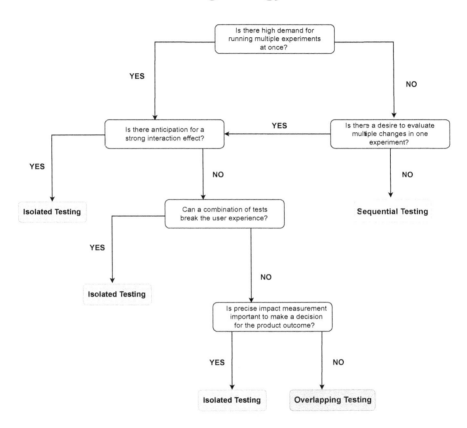

In the following Chapter Roundup, let's take a look at a few questions you can ponder to pinpoint the optimal testing strategy for your next project.

Chapter Roundup: What Type of Testing Strategy Best Suits Your Use Cases?

How you evaluate a product change is just as important as the when and why. Now that you're in tune with the different types of testing strategies, can you identify use cases from your past and future experiments that your product and engineering teams were eager to run that would lend themselves to either an isolated or overlapping experiment? Reflect on how these strategies might have influenced the speed of decision-making or the accuracy of your insights. Did a lack of clarity around the testing strategy ever lead to delays or misaligned priorities? Consider the following questions as you brainstorm.

- Is testing space availability a concern? If so, this should be an important factor when deciding which type of testing strategy to opt for.

- Is metric precision a priority? If it's important that you have test results that are accurate and not just a more general understanding of whether the impact was positive versus negative, then that plays a large role as to which type of testing strategy you leverage.

- Is coordination of experiments to run on the product roadmap top of mind? Or can tests run independently, not in order?

While you're answering the preceding questions, use the decision tree on page 47 to help in determining the ideal testing strategy.

Wrapping Up

You've just worked through the first of many strategies for leveling up your experimentation practice. At its core, an experimentation platform should make testing fast, efficient, and reliable—so teams can easily understand the impact of changes on key metrics. If testing feels slow or complicated, especially as demand grows, it's a sign that your tools and strategies may need to evolve.

As experimentation demand increases, coordination becomes increasingly important. Misaligned priorities or a lack of visibility into the testing pipeline can lead to bottlenecks and missed opportunities for learning. Revisiting strategies ensures that your platform evolves to meet the needs of growing teams and a more complex product landscape.

Here's a summary of what we covered:

- Explored testing strategies like isolated, overlapping, and sequential testing, understanding their advantages, limitations, and appropriate use cases.

- Learned how to implement overlapping tests effectively, enabling teams to run more experiments simultaneously without compromising data integrity.

- Visualized interaction effects to identify when overlapping tests are feasible and how to mitigate adverse user experiences.

- Identified signs of bottlenecks that suggest experimentation rate needs investment, such as limited testing space or long test durations.

- Introduced tooling solutions to improve coordination, visualize testing capacity, and plan experiments with greater ease and transparency.

- Outlined best practices for overlapping testing, including setting boundaries, monitoring metrics holistically, and educating teams on trade-offs.

- Emphasized testing guidelines to ensure platform resources are used efficiently and experiments align with product goals.

In the next chapter, you'll explore how test design influences experimentation rate and discover strategies to further optimize your platform's capacity for running high-quality experiments. Let's continue building your expertise to take your experimentation practices to the next level!

CHAPTER 3

Designing Better Experiments

Time and energy are finite resources. If you could do something with less effort, you'd be able to accomplish more. Running an A/B test for weeks and weeks is necessary at times, but what if you could design an experiment to require fewer resources? You'd likely be delighted with such an outcome—an experimentation dream perhaps.

The previous chapter covered different testing strategies—particularly those that help increase the number of experiments running in parallel. Adopting overlapping tests is one way to boost experimentation rate. Another key lever is improving experiment design to reduce the resources required to run a test, which is exactly where we'll turn our attention next.

We'll focus on the following:

- Leveraging top-line company-level metrics versus feature-level metrics.

- Reducing the number of test variants.

- Reviewing concepts that are core to experiment design.

- Creating a gold standard to ensure well-designed experiments are launched on the product.

- Implementing the capping metrics technique to reduce variance.

To continue scaling and advancing your experimentation practices, the next step is to design experiments that are resource-efficient while still delivering reliable, trustworthy insights. This chapter will show you how.

Improving Experiment Design

Let's say you decide to cook more meals at home instead of opting for takeout. However, you're a busy person; if cooking dinner takes hours, you're more likely to get takeout. Getting takeout isn't the healthiest of habits, so figuring out how to cook meals efficiently at home is worth optimizing. Now, let's apply this to experimentation. If your experimentation design is overly complicated or time-consuming, it becomes less effective as a tool for evaluating product ideas and changes. Teams might be tempted to bypass this critical step, risking decisions based on guesswork rather than data. Just like efficient cooking supports healthier habits, streamlining experimentation ensures it remains an integral part of a healthy product development life cycle.

The design, or anatomy, of an experiment directly influences the execution time and insights validity. Check out the image below illustrating the key factors in designing a good A/B test. From setting the experiment objective to the duration to the sample size of each variant, these factors are all important to designing effective experiments.

Good experiment design is crucial for ensuring that your results are valid, reliable, and actionable. A clear definition of the experiment's objective or hypothesis is foundational. If you're uncertain about what you're trying to learn, your choice of metrics may be misaligned. Likewise, an unclear goal will affect decisions around test duration and the number of variants. It's essential to define your goal early in the experiment design process so you can choose appropriate metrics and calculate the necessary sample size to detect meaningful differences between variants with sufficient statistical power.

An often-overlooked element of experiment design is simplicity. Experiments that are overly complex or difficult to execute can introduce operational challenges, such as misconfigurations or delays in launching. By designing experiments that are straightforward to implement and monitor, teams can reduce friction in the testing process and increase the overall velocity of experimentation. This streamlined approach not only ensures high-quality insights but also encourages teams to rely more heavily on experimentation as a reliable tool for decision-making.

Let's start with creating a gold standard for teams to aim for when designing experiments.

Defining the Gold Standard

A gold standard for A/B testing is like having a trusted recipe—it ensures consistency, accuracy, and confidence, leading to more reliable and actionable results. Clear guidelines for setting up experiments and interpreting results reduce the risk of flawed tests while giving teams the clarity they need to design trustworthy experiments.

Let's be honest: many teams running experiments won't instinctively know all the details required for a well-designed test—and that's perfectly fine. The key is to lower the barriers to this knowledge by creating an easy-to-follow gold standard that anyone can rely on. As you introduce more advanced strategies into your experimentation playbook, having this foundation becomes even more critical. A clear and accessible gold standard ensures that experiments remain consistent, insightful, and dependable, no matter how complex your methodologies become.

So what does a gold standard look like in practice? At its core, it defines the essential conditions for effective A/B testing, which, as shown in the following illustration, fall into two main categories: experiment configuration and product experience.

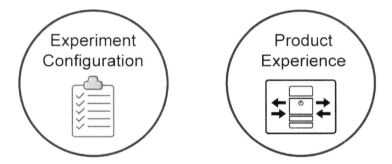

Good experimental design includes all of the factors defined on on page 52. If all of these attributes are defined correctly, then your experiment meets the gold standard from a configuration lens.

Experiment configuration involves ensuring that all aspects of the test setup are optimized for accuracy and statistical validity. This includes proper randomization, sufficient sample size, and clear definitions of control and variant groups. It also requires identifying the right primary and secondary metrics to evaluate success as well as setting thresholds for statistical significance and confidence intervals. A well-configured experiment eliminates common pitfalls like biased traffic allocation or inadequate power, which can compromise the integrity of the results.

The product experience category has prerequisites that are contextual to the product in which the A/B test is executed on, such as crucial UX components or features essential to the business that should always be available. For instance, in a subscription model product, components like upsell buttons between subscription tiers and an Account Details page to inform users about their subscription features are critical for a valid user experience. The product experience must be valid before deeming an experiment ready for launch. This involves minimizing disruption to the user journey, ensuring that changes are meaningful and measurable, and avoiding scenarios where overlapping tests might create confusion or interaction effects.

By splitting the gold standard into two categories—experiment configuration and product experience—teams can get a clearer picture of both the technical setup and the user-facing product experience that make an A/B test successful. Keeping these standards in one central place, like an experimentation playbook, makes it easy for new team members to get up to speed and follow best practices.

To illustrate further, let's see what it looks like to define the gold standard for running experiments on the MarketMax product in your next Engineer Task.

Engineer Task: Defining a Gold Standard

The MarketMax experimentation team wants to create a gold standard for ensuring the testing capacity is used effectively by always running well-designed, reliable experiments on the product.

As an engineer on the experimentation platform team, what criteria would you set to ensure teams meet the gold standard for running experiments on the product? Remember, the product is a website where customers can buy craft goods that were created by small businesses or local artists. Defining these criteria should include requirements from both the lens of the test configuration and also the product experience. For example, consider components that should always be present in the MarketMax website to maintain the holistic product experience.

 Engineer Task: What requirements should be defined in the gold standard for running experiments at MarketMax?

First, let's define elements to address requirements for the test definition. Fundamental components of an A/B test, such as guardrail metrics to monitor the product holistically and targeting criteria for the test and control variants, is a great example of what should be included in your gold standard definition. More specifically, a well-designed test should have the following:

1. Hypothesis
2. Success and guardrail metrics
3. Targeting criteria
4. Duration
5. Power analysis
6. Sample size

The hypothesis is a key required element so anyone can understand the intent of the experiment. Success and guardrail metrics are needed to measure the effect of the change in comparison to the control. The targeting criteria influence the users allocated to the test and control variants. Power analysis calculates the required sample size to detect meaningful differences, and the duration dictates how long the test should run to collect sufficient data. All of these attributes of a test's design should be included in the gold standard definition to ensure teams are running high-quality experiments. It should also be clear how teams can accurately set the right values for each element—for instance, examples of how to define the duration in relation to the metrics and power analysis, or a table that illustrates critical guardrail metrics for each area of the product. Teams should also understand that sample size isn't an infinite resource—their test design directly affects how efficiently those resources are used. Poorly scoped experiments with unnecessary variants or weak hypotheses can waste valuable sample, delaying learnings and limiting testing opportunities for others. A well-designed test helps teams make the most of the sample they have, speeding up iteration and maximizing the value of every experiment run.

Now, let's define conditions for product experience by identifying key components that should be present holistically on the product. See the image shown on page 56 to define the parts of the product that must be present for the experiment to be considered a valid user experience from a business and product point of view.

For example, the shopping cart icon should be available on every page so users can easily access or order their craft goods. Similarly, links to critical features—such as search, past orders, the personalized home page, and account information—must remain intact. From the business perspective, there may also be strict requirements, like ensuring promotional sales

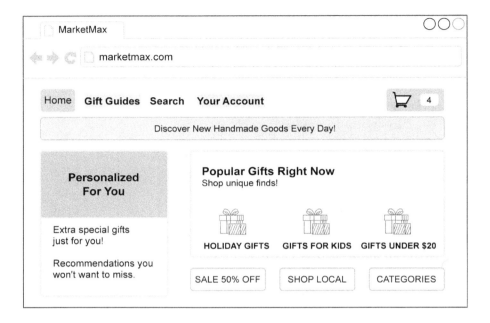

recommendations are always visible on the home page. If these core components are missing in an experiment setup, the user experience is incomplete, and any insights derived from the test would be unreliable for decision-making.

Having guidelines for teams to meet the gold standard for experimentation on the product will result in higher-quality insights, fewer issues, and greater trust in the experimentation practices.

Let's switch gears to another tactic that influences the design of a test—metrics!

Opting for Sensitive Metrics

Imagine you're baking a cake, but instead of checking the cake's texture or taste to see if it's baked correctly, you decide to track how much the cake rises in the oven. At first, this might seem like a good approach—more rise might mean it's baking well, right? However, focusing only on how much the cake rises ignores other important factors, like whether it's fully cooked or tastes good. You might end up with a cake that looks good on the outside but is undercooked inside (yikes).

Translating this metaphor to experimentation, choosing the right metrics is crucial. Focusing on the wrong measurements or those that take too long to reveal meaningful differences can prolong your experiment unnecessarily.

Suppose you're conducting lengthy experiments but have limited testing time. In that case, selecting more sensitive metrics that provide quicker insights into the effectiveness of the changes introduced to a subset of users may be better.

Metric sensitivity plays a significant role in your experiment design. The more sensitive a metric is, the more likely the metric will change, given the feature evaluated in the experiment's scope. If you've selected a success metric that does not align with your experiment hypothesis, it'll be much harder to measure the effect of the change evaluated in the test.

Metrics like short-term engagement or task completion rates can often provide directional signals much faster than longer-term outcomes like retention or lifetime value. While these quick-to-move metrics might not capture the full picture, they can act as proxies that allow you to evaluate whether a change is worth pursuing further in a longer-term experiment.

If you're unsure which metrics would be more sensitive given the change you're evaluating in the scope of an A/B test, consider classifying your metrics into one of these two categories: company top-line metrics and feature metrics.

Company top-line metrics measure key performance of the product at a higher level, such as retention, user satisfaction, monthly active users (MAU), monthly consumption hours, and daily active users (DAU). These metrics closely align with the company's business model. To effectively evaluate if a change impacts company top-line metrics, you'll likely need to run the test longer to see the effect, or measure using longer-term experiments such as holdbacks. In general, company top-line metrics are harder to move—not impossible, but harder. It's also important to consider big feature launches and marketing campaign timelines if you're measuring experiment success with top-line metrics, as they may be influenced by other factors.

Feature metrics are closer to a team's area of influence on the product and are typically more sensitive. It depends on the feature and product offering, but the most common feature-level metrics include click-through rate, transaction rate, or feature revisit rate. See the diagram shown on page 58.

At this point, you may think that feature metrics aren't as important as company metrics. Who cares about the click-through rate of a feature on a website? User retention is what matters. On the contrary, what if a user continually clicks or engages with a feature on a website? Then they become more likely to build a repeat habit and, on a longer timeline, transition to a daily active user. That would be great, right?

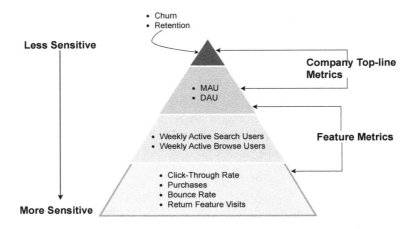

Said otherwise, feature metrics should causally relate to your company's top-line metrics. See the following image.

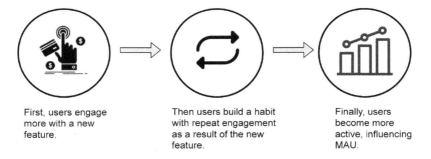

| First, users engage more with a new feature. | Then users build a habit with repeat engagement as a result of the new feature. | Finally, users become more active, influencing MAU. |

Now, let's assume you've selected the right metric for your experiment. To quantify the sensitivity of your metric, you'll want to consider a couple of factors. First, calculate the statistical power to define the success metric's Minimal Detectable Effect (MDE). You'll rely on the MDE to understand whether the metric is sensitive enough to move in either a positive or negative direction when used to measure the effect of a change on the product. Second, analyze movement probability to ensure the metric will change such that the results are deemed statistically significant.

By improving metric sensitivity for your experiments, you can detect smaller differences more efficiently using smaller sample sizes. Smaller sample sizes should also influence your ramp-up time, making for a shorter incremental ramp-up schedule if fewer users are assigned to an experiment.

Testing design tweaks like this has an impact on the process of running experiments on a product. By improving metric sensitivity, optimizing statistical power, and adjusting sample sizes, you can significantly improve experimentation practices. All of these examples entail some degree of fine-tuning, so leaning on your trusty data scientist is key.

For more information on metric sensitivity, read the article titled "Beyond Power Analysis: Metric Sensitivity Analysis in A/B Tests."[1]

Zooming In on Minimal Detectable Effect

At the heart of measuring metric sensitivity is the concept of *minimal detectable effect* (MDE), a foundational element in experimentation. The MDE represents the smallest effect size (or change in a metric) that an experiment is designed to detect, given a specific sample size, statistical power, and significance level. In simpler terms, it's the smallest change that would be considered meaningful enough to take action on and that the experiment can reliably detect.

While this book focuses on making advanced experimentation concepts approachable and practical, we've generally steered clear of diving deep into statistical formulas. After all, plenty of resources out there already break down the math side of things. But given how important MDE is, it's worth taking a moment to understand the variables involved. See the following image for the formula to compute MDE.

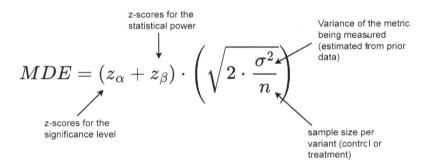

In practice, MDE provides a guideline for both sample size and sensitivity. A smaller MDE requires a larger sample size or a lower standard deviation in the metric, both of which influence the precision and detectability of results.

Why Does MDE Matter?

MDE is critical because it directly influences the design of your experiment:

---

1.   https://www.microsoft.com/en-us/research/articles/beyond-power-analysis-metric-sensitivity-in-a-b-tests/

- *Experiment duration.* A smaller MDE often requires more users to detect subtle effects, which can extend the test's duration.

- *Sample size.* A larger sample size reduces variability, making it easier to detect small effects but may not always be feasible.

- *Decision-making.* If your MDE is too large, you might miss smaller, meaningful improvements. Conversely, if it's too small, you risk overinvesting resources in detecting changes that might not have significant business impact.

Let's revisit the idea of metric sensitivity through the lens of MDE. Metrics with high variability (for example, revenue) will naturally have a larger MDE, while metrics with lower variability (click-through rates, for example) can achieve a smaller MDE. This makes certain metrics more sensitive and practical for short-term experimentation.

Illustrating MDE at MarketMax

Let's say MarketMax is testing a new recommendation algorithm. The team's primary goal is to increase click-through rates (CTR). Here's how MDE comes into play:

- Current CTR: 5%
- Target CTR increase: +0.5%
- Standard deviation of CTR: 1.5%
- Desired power: 80% (z-score = 0.84)
- Significance level: 95% (z-score = 1.96)

Using the MDE formula, the team calculates the sample size needed to reliably detect a 0.5% increase in CTR. If the required sample size is too large to test within the desired timeline, they may either increase the test duration, lower the confidence level, or reconsider using a more sensitive metric to gauge success.

Bringing It Back to Metric Sensitivity

MDE underscores the importance of metric sensitivity when designing experiments. By improving metric sensitivity—choosing metrics with lower variability or designing experiments to reduce variance—you can achieve smaller MDEs. This enables faster, more efficient tests that require fewer users while still producing actionable results.

For example, if your goal is to measure the revenue impact of a feature, you could consider proxy metrics like average transaction size or add-to-cart rates, which are often more sensitive and have lower variability. These metrics can provide earlier signals, allowing you to evaluate changes without needing massive sample sizes or long experiment durations.

Leveraging the Capping Metric Technique

Now that you know how to choose the right metric, you can leverage the capping metric technique to improve statistical power. By capping metrics, you can limit the influence of unusually high or low data points that might otherwise distort the measurement of an effect, especially when working with highly variable metrics.

The capping metrics technique involves setting upper (and sometimes lower) limits (also referred to as thresholds) on the values of specific metrics to reduce the impact of extreme outliers. Outliers can skew test results, so reducing their impact is important. With capping, you gain a more representative estimate of the effect of the changes you're evaluating in an A/B test, as the analysis focuses on the broader, more typical user base rather than rare extreme behaviors.

The benefits of capping your metrics include the following:

- Reducing variance
- Focusing on common usage behavior
- Avoiding skewed results

Extreme values often don't represent typical user behavior and may not be as relevant to the overall outcome you're testing. By capping, you concentrate the analysis on common behaviors, making insights more actionable and applicable to most users.

Let's consider an example use case at MarketMax. Imagine an A/B test where the intent is to measure the revenue impact of a new UX design on the purchase flow as a user adds craft goods to their cart. If a small number of users make substantial purchases, these outliers could inflate the average revenue per user, masking the true effect. By capping revenue at a certain threshold, you ensure the test reflects the impact on a broader, more representative sample set. As a side note, it's worth examining the user sessions for those cases where a large number of purchases were made—it may lead to interesting product insights and could potentially uncover a user cohort worth further investing in if, for example, they are more likely to purchase craft goods compared to the average user.

To further illustrate what capping metrics looks like in practice, see the step-by-step diagram shown on page 62.

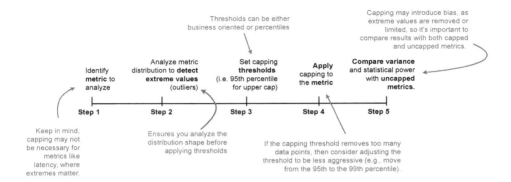

By capping outlier values, you reduce the variance in the metric, making it easier to detect meaningful differences. Lower variance in the metric increases the experiment's statistical power, enabling the detection of smaller effects.

Deciding When to Use Capping

While capping is a powerful technique, it's best to know when you should employ it. Use cases that clearly support capping metrics include the following:

- *Managing highly variable metrics.* Revenue, time spent, and the number of items purchased often show significant variance due to outliers.

- *Ensuring representativeness.* If your experiment's goal is to evaluate the impact on the majority of users, capping can help you narrow in on the analysis of the typical users.

- *Excluding irrelevant extreme values.* If outliers are unrelated to the change being tested, capping ensures they don't dominate the results.

Don't ignore what outliers might reveal; they can often point to unique opportunities for growth or areas needing further investigation. You can always do a separate analysis for outliers while maintaining uncapped metrics.

Reducing Variance to Improve Statistical Power

One of the key advantages of capping outlier values is the reduction in metric variance. High variance in metrics increases the sample size required to detect statistically significant differences, potentially prolonging your experiment. By reducing variance through capping, you enhance the statistical power of the test, enabling the detection of smaller, meaningful effects within a shorter time frame.

For example, in an experiment measuring average session duration, users who leave the app open for hours without interacting might skew results. Capping session duration at a reasonable threshold can help align the metric more closely with active engagement, reducing noise and increasing the sensitivity of the experiment.

We'll explore more advanced (and more complicated) variance reduction strategies later in this chapter. In the meantime, keep in mind that this technique is one of the simpler implementations in the variance reduction realm. You do run the risk of introducing bias, but that doesn't necessarily mean you should avoid the technique altogether. You can employ strategies to combat bias-variance, such as creating multiple levels of capping—that is, 1%, 1.5%, 2%, and so on. By having multiple capped metrics, you can compare and study the variances.

Aligning on Experiment Goal

The number one rule of A/B testing is simple. Ensure you can answer this question: what are you trying to learn from the experiment?

Sometimes you aim to detect a positive effect in metrics by introducing a specific change to your users. Other evaluations may aim to ensure a change is non-inferior, no worse than the control given a predefined margin. If you're having difficulty defining the objective for evaluating a change in the scope of an experiment, consider categorizing your test into one of the following categories:

1. *Test to derisk.* The experiment's goal is to reduce the risk of degrading the user experience or introducing poor-performing system changes to all your users at once.

2. *Test to learn.* The experiment's goal is to learn more about the change or prototype to inform future product development and give you the confidence to continue investing beyond the initial prototype. You'll configure smaller sample ratios and feature-level metrics in your test design, decreasing the time it takes to gain initial insights.

3. *Test to measure.* The experiment's goal is to compute how a change impacts your user, product, and business metrics that are more sensitive. Since your objective is to understand the impact before potentially enabling the feature for all users, you can also refer to this category as "test to launch."

4. *Test to measure long-term impact.* The experiment's goal is to measure the effect of a feature or change on longer-term metrics, such as retention, churn, and monthly active users.

Each test category has a distinct goal, so aligning on the objective is critical before configuring the experiment, as the goal does influence the test design.

The following image illustrates the hierarchy of test categories in relation to their general duration, a key factor of experiment design.

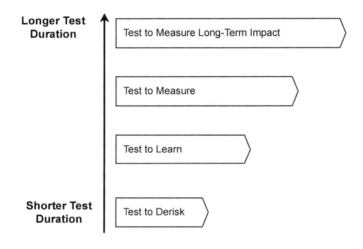

In the spirit of reducing testing duration, experiments with the goal of learning and derisking can be shorter, which makes them very attractive if the goal is to gain early insights. A test to learn should not have the same metrics as a test to measure, as your goal is to gain early insights into the idea's validity and not necessarily understand company-level impact. Keep in mind that after conducting a test to learn, you should run a test to measure the impact on key metrics with higher significance.

A typical example of a test to learn is when you're at the beginning stages of prototyping a new feature that requires early insights to gauge the product and design team's initial instincts on the overall design. In this case, a practical next step is a shorter experiment to conduct ad-hoc analysis and understand user engagement (with feature-level metrics) at a smaller scale with less statistical significance.

As for the test-to-derisk category, there are also use cases where a non-user-facing change is A/B tested to understand latency and response time effects. When measuring engineering performance in the scope of an experiment, your goal is to derisk a change that could cause an incident or outage. By enabling the change for a subset of users, you'll gain more confidence before it's available for all users. A test to derisk can be shorter if the metrics aren't product-oriented, as your goal is to capture sufficient data to understand system-level metrics.

If the goal is to increase confidence but not necessarily measure the exact effect in a statistically significant way, then opting for a shorter-duration test where the intent is to derisk or learn is a great option to increase your experimentation rate. Now that you can use the four testing categories, let's consider another solution that impacts testing design.

Reducing the Number of Variants

Imagine you are a chef preparing a multicourse meal. If you try to cook all the dishes at the same time—juggling different ingredients, temperatures, and cooking times—you're likely to end up spending more time in the kitchen and might even risk undercooking or burning some dishes. On the other hand, if you focus on one or two dishes at a time, you can control the process better.

This is similar to configuring an experiment. A basic experiment involves a test variant and a control variant. You can introduce multiple test variants, like adding more dishes to your cooking. However, the more variants you include, the longer it will take to reach the desired level of statistical significance. By reducing the number of variants, you'll directly reduce the sample size or duration of the test. And remember: sample size isn't an unlimited resource.

Let's illustrate evaluating multiple variants and how that impacts experiment design with an example test at MarketMax.

Evaluating Model Features at MarketMax

A common use case for evaluating multiple test variants in one experiment is in the context of machine learning models, specifically feature weights. A feature is data that's used as input to the machine learning model so that it can produce predictions. A model can apply varying degrees of weight to a feature to define its importance; the larger the weight, the more important that feature is.

At MarketMax, the Search team is deciding how to define the weight of a new feature—user location—in their search relevancy model. They choose to run an A/B test to determine the most effective weight for the user location feature that correlates to improved product metrics. See the following image.

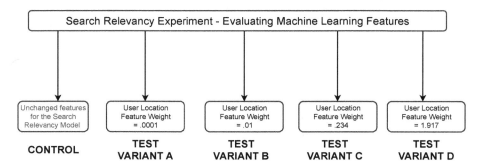

Testing multiple variants in one experiment is a tactic often used by the Search team. The advantage of evaluating more than one variant at once is that you get more data insights from a single experiment.

On the other hand, the disadvantage of running a multivariate test is that it requires testing resources. Specifically, more time is needed to QA each variant's configuration. Also, more time is needed for the actual duration of the test, and more users are required to reach significance. Of course, in a perfect world, resource constraints would never be a concern when running A/B tests on a product. However, that's rarely the case, so let's continue this discussion by exploring the impact of having multiple test variants in the upcoming Engineer Task.

Engineer Task: Impact of Multiple Test Variants

The MarketMax experiment that we recently reviewed evaluating multiple variants, on page 66, aims to determine the optimal weight for the new user location feature in the search relevancy model. The ideal weight could be 0.0001 (Variant A) or 0.234 (Variant C). Why do you think having five test variants to evaluate within one experiment could increase the duration?

 Engineer Task: What is the impact of designing an experiment with five test variants?

Testing multiple variants simultaneously requires a larger user base. The more variants you test, the more users you need to accurately measure the impact and draw reliable conclusions. For example, if an experiment requires more users than the website's monthly traffic, the test design should account for this. Ending the test prematurely, without reaching the necessary user count, will lead to metrics that don't accurately reflect the true effect.

You can combat the need to test five distinct variants in one experiment in various ways. Sometimes, you can defer to offline evaluations to filter out lower-performing configurations, especially when evaluating a machine learning model. If the Search team conducted an offline assessment of each feature weight and its impact on the model's predictions using an offline metric, such as recall or normalized discounted cumulative gain (NDCG), they could reduce the number of variants tested in the online experiment.

Leveraging the interleaving strategy is another method that can decrease the number of users needed to evaluate a change, especially with machine learning models that are used for ranking search or browse results. This foreshadows Chapter 4, Improving Machine Learning Evaluation Practices, on page 75, where we'll explore both interleaving and offline evaluations to increase the rate of algorithmic-oriented A/B tests.

Next, we'll explore a common algorithmic technique used to remove variances in metrics using historical data.

Reducing Up-Front Sample Size with CUPED

Variance reduction is a powerful technique that can strengthen your experimentation strategy by improving your ability to detect small changes in metrics. By boosting the sensitivity to subtle effects, you can make more confident decisions faster or with smaller sample sizes, shaping your experiment design while ensuring reliable insights.

When you reduce variability, even subtle changes evaluated in an A/B test can be detected—changes that might otherwise go unnoticed without a variance reduction strategy. The concept of powering an experiment is often the biggest struggle; if the power is too low, your experiment may fail to detect a meaningful effect even if one exists. Conversely, if the power is too high, you may over-sample unnecessarily, wasting time and resources. Variance reduction techniques help ensure that your experiment is well powered without requiring excessive sample sizes, enabling efficient and accurate decision-making.

One of the most common variance reduction techniques is Controlled Experiment Using Preexperiment Data (CUPED). CUPED uses preexperiment, historical data to reduce variance in metrics during the experiment. This historical data is collected prior to the start of the experiment and helps improve the precision of the results.

CUPED can be used to reduce up-front sample size, as the covariate coefficients can be estimated from the historical data. If you don't have access to historical data, then CUPED isn't a strategy to pursue, as it's a foundational element.

In practice, three critical steps are required to implement CUPED:

1. Identify covariates.
2. Adjust the outcome metric using statistical methods.
3. Incorporate adjustment after the experiment ends.

A covariate is a variable that can correlate with the success metric in an experiment. For example, if you're measuring transaction rates on the MarketMax website, then a covariate would be historical transaction-rate behavior. Defining the covariate is a key step in the CUPED methodology, so you want to ensure you're defining a good covariate. In most cases, good covariates can correlate well with the metric you're measuring in your A/B test.

Once you've identified your covariates, a researcher or data scientist should implement an adjustment calculation to account for the variability in the metric for each user allocated to the experiment. In other words, you're implementing statistical functions to adjust the outcome metric to reduce noise in the data and get more accurate insights on the effect.

Finally, as the experiment concludes, incorporate the covariate adjustment into your data analysis to detect the true impact of the feature evaluated in the scope of an A/B test.

The two classic methods for implementing CUPED are stratification and covariates. Both methods require similar data and have a common goal of exploiting this preexperiment historical data to control variation in the test. Plenty of resources are available to dive deeper into the theory behind the CUPED method. In particular, check out the paper titled "Improving the sensitivity of online controlled experiments by utilizing pre-experiment data."[2]

The most common use cases that benefit from CUPED is when the effects of a change are subtle, as it helps to ensure that these effects are not lost in the noise of unrelated variability. For instance, the user has to click a specific button to engage with the new feature or navigate to a specific page within an application. In this case, measuring a true treatment effect is difficult because fewer users will experience the new feature being evaluated as part of the test variant.

---

2. https://dl.acm.org/doi/abs/10.1145/2433396.2433413

Being able to measure incremental improvements on a product is important, and with variance reduction strategies, you can detect smaller effect sizes and end A/B tests more quickly, effectively improving your experimentation rate.

With all these strategies top of mind, let's see what's needed to ensure teams are aware of the many tools within the experimentation tool kit.

Sharing Experimentation Best Practices

A/B testing platforms are like hammers; the end result depends on the skill of the person wielding it. Just as even the best tools require skilled craftsmanship to build something meaningful, the success of an A/B testing platform depends on how well teams are equipped to use it. The most advanced platform won't deliver impactful results if the people using it lack the knowledge or support to design and execute effective experiments.

To ensure teams can adopt the various tactics outlined in this chapter and maximize the value of the platform, three key components are essential: documentation, workshops, and tooling. Together, these elements provide the structure, education, and support necessary to enable consistent, high-quality experimentation across an organization. Without them, teams may struggle to navigate the complexities of advanced testing strategies, leading to inefficiencies, poor-quality experiments, and missed opportunities for learning.

First, let's explore why documentation is key.

Writing Documentation to Promote Best Practices

An indicator that may suggest your experimentation practices need more documentation is if teams are constantly messaging or reaching out to the platform team for questions on how to run a test. The better your documentation is, the less your team should have to engage with users of the platform. Of course, there will always be questions, but there shouldn't be an excessive amount related to the basic steps for designing an experiment.

If a method or strategy exists on your experimentation platform that influences how a team could design a test, it's essential to detail which scenarios benefit from them and which don't through documentation. If you didn't know something existed, how would you learn to use it? Similarly, teams are unlikely to leverage a specific strategy if the information is siloed or inaccessible. Without documentation, teams could run tests longer than necessary or use an approach that doesn't give them the user insights they need.

It's common for product and engineering teams to ignore the experimentation design step and expect it to work as simply as possible. The experimentation platform and teams that support experimentation practices at your company should advocate for and encourage better test design through detailed documentation.

Now you may be thinking experimentation best practices and a gold standard are the same. They aren't the same. A gold standard is the essential elements for a well-structured, reliable, and statistically sound experiment—including configuration and product elements. Your gold standard defines the design elements that must be met for any experiment to be valid. On the other hand, the experimentation best practices include guidance on how and when to use each of the distinct strategies available for teams that run experiments on the product. The best practices document should be similar to a practical playbook for teams.

Running A/B Testing Workshops

Most people with an espresso machine in their kitchen weren't initially experts at making fancy lattes. It took time, practice, and many tutorials to go from instant coffee to a cappuccino. Similarly, the teams that run A/B tests on a product aren't typically experimentation experts; they often need clear direction on which strategy to use and when.

Suppose a product engineering team configuring an experiment is entirely unaware of how to configure an experiment. In that case, they won't know how to run an effective test that can lead to a decision on whether the feature should be shipped to product for all users to engage with. This is where workshops can play a significant role in up-leveling other teams' A/B testing domain knowledge.

For example, concepts such as identifying which type of test, whether it's a test to learn or a test to derisk, and how the test design should alter depending on the type of test, could be included in an experimentation workshop.

Providing guidance through hands-on workshops will get you closer to your users of the experimentation platform and potentially serve as an informal user feedback session where you may hear specific pain points when running experiments on the product. As you hear these pain points, consider implementing tooling to resolve them. This leads us to the next tip that can increase adoption of these experimentation practices.

Implementing Tooling to Support Best Practices

Building tools that simplify the process of running experiments is a central theme throughout this book. Just as we discussed in Chapter 1, Why Experimentation Rate, Quality, and Cost Matter, on page 1, where we explore a tool designed to capture space availability issues; you can incorporate similar functionality into your experimentation platform to help users optimize their test configurations.

For example, if you have validators built into the platform that check for top-line metrics in the success metric field of a test configuration, you could alert the team that they could consider a more sensitive metric to evaluate the feature's effect on the product.

Another useful feature might be a field in the test configuration tool that states if the test's primary objective is to learn, derisk, or launch. By encouraging teams to specify their intent, this field could help them align their test design with their strategic goals, ensuring they run the most suitable type of experiment for their evaluation.

The hard truth of building experimentation platforms is that adoption doesn't happen overnight. Even with better strategies available, teams won't immediately shift from long, data-heavy tests to shorter, more efficient designs—especially if those approaches feel unfamiliar. That's why it's worth investing in clear documentation, thoughtful workshops, and strong tooling. When teams have access to real examples and case studies, the path to adoption becomes much smoother.

Ultimately, the goal is to make it easy for teams to design experiments that generate user insights and inform product decisions. Even the most advanced experimentation platforms depend on clear documentation to uphold best practices.

Now that you have all these strategies in your tool kit to improve experimentation rate, let's move on to the Chapter Roundup.

Chapter Roundup: Identifying Experiment Design Improvements

To practice the concepts discussed in this chapter, reflect on experiments you've executed in the past. Can you think of examples where a variance reduction strategy would have impacted the product outcome? Or consider experiments you plan on running in the future: could you opt for more sensitive feature-level metrics?

Use the following questions to help you identify experiments that could benefit from some of the techniques illustrated in this chapter:

- Are you evaluating back-end or architectural changes that aren't visible to the user? If so, a shorter experiment duration should provide enough data to understand the impact on engineering system metrics by running a test to derisk.

- Are you evaluating a machine learning model with multiple test variants? If so, can you leverage offline evaluations to filter down the number of test variants in the A/B test and therefore decrease the sample size required to power all test variants?

- Are you building a prototype to learn more about the new feature? Is your goal to get initial data insights but not necessarily evaluate the specific impact on metrics? If so, this would be considered a test to learn more about the feature in a production setting.

Wrapping Up

Strong experiment design on product that has a high demand for running experiments isn't just about getting insights, it's about getting the right insights, faster and with fewer resources. In this chapter, you took important steps toward making your experiments more thoughtful, efficient, and scalable.

Here's a quick recap of what we covered:

- Defined the categories of experiments and how they influence duration and sample size, from quick tests to derisk changes to longer tests for measuring long-term impacts.

- Explored practical strategies for optimizing test design, such as reducing the number of test variants to save time and resources.

- Outlined the gold standard for experiments to ensure all tests meet high-quality requirements from both technical and user experience perspectives.

- Introduced the capping metrics technique as a simple yet effective way to reduce variance and improve the sensitivity of metrics.

- Detailed how CUPED can be used to reduce up-front sample size, as you can estimate the covariate coefficients using historical data (a key element required to implement CUPED).

Each of these strategies equips you to design experiments that are resource-efficient while still delivering actionable insights. Next, we'll explore the popular domain of machine learning and its intersection with A/B testing for evaluating algorithmic effectiveness in user-facing products.

CHAPTER 4

Improving Machine Learning Evaluation Practices

Open your phone and glance at your recently used apps. Chances are at least one of them is powered by machine learning—whether it's a recommendation algorithm filtering content in your news feed or a model suggesting TV shows to watch. Whatever the use case, measuring the impact of these machine learning features on product performance, business outcomes, and user experience is absolutely essential.

From the previous chapter, you know that it's important to consider your experiment design and the ways to decrease resources needed to run an experiment, such as fewer test variants or leveraging more sensitive metrics.

In this chapter, the focus will still be on increasing experimentation rate, but hyper-focus on strategies that can help you measure the impact of machine learning models on a product. More specifically, we'll explore the following:

- How to leverage offline evaluations to increase insights before the A/B testing stage.

- How to incorporate a multi-arm bandit algorithm in place of traditional experiments.

- How to implement interleaving for ranking algorithm evaluations.

Now that you know what's in store for this chapter, let's gradient descend into the details.

Identifying Challenges with Machine Learning

Building products that use machine learning to improve the user experience is an industry standard. Leveraging machine learning on any product is a time investment in comparison to features that rely on simple heuristics or straightforward business logic.

Machine learning models take time to develop and test. With machine learning, you're not just creating complex models; you're also developing the systems that support features dependent on the model's output. These systems encompass training pipelines, data pipelines, deployment infrastructure, serving infrastructure, and monitoring frameworks. Clearly, a lot goes into supporting machine learning in a production setting.

Aside from the vast systems and infrastructure, the development life cycle for a machine learning model includes an additional offline evaluation step. Offline evaluations for a machine learning model are used to measure performance before the predictions or output are available for users in an online experimentation setting. See the following image.

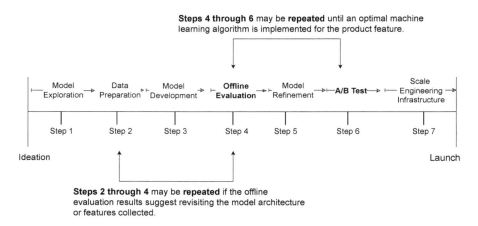

As depicted in the development process, it's likely that steps will be repeated based on the outcomes observed between the offline and online evaluation phases. This repetition naturally extends the time needed to evaluate a model before it's enabled for all users of a product.

Let's explore some challenges at MarketMax to highlight the pain points in the machine learning development process.

Engineer Task: Identifying Challenges Within the Machine Learning Development Process

Focusing on the machine learning development process that's illustrated on page 76, what challenges do you foresee MarketMax engineering and product teams facing when developing features dependent on machine learning? Are teams concerned about the time required to measure a model's impact in both offline and online evaluation stages? Or are there other, more nuanced challenges, such as having the right metrics to measure effect?

 Engineer Task: What challenges exist in the machine learning process at MarketMax?

Considering the experimentation platform survey results on page 15, increasing the number of experiments with conclusive results might have been top of mind for you. At MarketMax, 37 percent of experiments resulted in inefficient data for the team to make a decision, and since the feedback loop for machine learning models is so high, learning as much as you can earlier in the development cycle is ideal. Offline evaluations are one tactic that teams can lean on to better understand the effect before running an A/B test.

Another challenge is enabling teams to repeatedly conduct offline evaluations each time the model is refined or updated, without adding significant overhead. From a platform perspective, the opportunity lies in building a robust and scalable offline evaluation system that allows anyone to run evaluations at any time. The easier it is to execute an offline evaluation for your model, the more likely you will identify factors or areas for improvement before users are exposed to the model's predictions.

Introducing a complex model into production with minimal impact on key metrics is a mistake. The complexity of machine learning must offer a higher value proposition than simpler solutions, so it's critical that you have all of the right strategies to measure effectiveness.

It's worth taking a quick tangent here, as it relates to machine learning. While much of this book focuses on increasing testing capacity, having the capability doesn't mean you shouldn't be judicious with your online testing capacity. If you have the right tools to measure potential effects beforehand, make full use of them before entering the online experimentation stage. In the case of machine learning, you can learn a lot in the offline stage before you expose users to the model in the product. Offline evaluations cannot replace online experiments for uncovering true user and product impacts, but they can shape your experimental design and help mitigate the risk of deploying underperforming variants.

In the case of machine learning, the offline stage provides a unique opportunity to learn about your model's performance in a controlled and risk-free environment. Offline evaluations allow you to assess key metrics like precision, recall, ranking effectiveness, and error rates using historical datasets, all of which we'll discuss further in an upcoming section. These evaluations also enable you to iterate on hyperparameters, fine-tune features, and debug edge cases before the model ever interacts with live users.

While offline evaluations cannot fully replace the necessity of online experimentation—since only live testing can reveal the true impact on user behavior and product metrics—they are capable of increasing insights and reducing risks. By identifying poor-performing variants and potential issues early, you minimize the likelihood of exposing users to suboptimal experiences. This protects your users and also ensures that your online experimentation bandwidth is used more effectively.

In machine learning, a thoughtful balance between offline and online evaluations is key to optimizing your development cycle. Offline evaluations offer a cost-effective and scalable way to filter, refine, and validate models, while online experiments provide the final, real-world validation necessary to measure user and product impact. Together, they form a complementary system that enables informed decision-making and reduces the risk of introducing poorly performing variants into your product ecosystem.

Let's see how you can increase insights earlier in the development stages of your machine learning model by leveraging offline evaluations.

Measuring Effect with Offline Methods

Imagine you're a chef trying to perfect a new recipe. You want to make sure it will be a hit, so before serving it to paying customers, you decide to do a taste test in your own kitchen. By taste-testing the new recipe in your kitchen, you'll catch obvious mistakes, such as too much salt, before serving it in a real-world setting. Once you're confident the recipe is reasonable based on your taste tests, you introduce it for a limited time to customers to gauge affinity for the new recipe.

Similar to tasting a new recipe in your own kitchen before serving it to guests, evaluating machine learning models begins with offline metrics that simulate performance without real user exposure. These metrics help identify potential issues and provide valuable insights early, reducing the risk of deploying poorly performing models. The following flowchart illustrates this progression—represented as a kitchen taste test—starting with offline evaluation, moving to online A/B testing to gather real customer feedback, and ultimately leading to full deployment, akin to serving the new recipe as part of the main dinner menu.

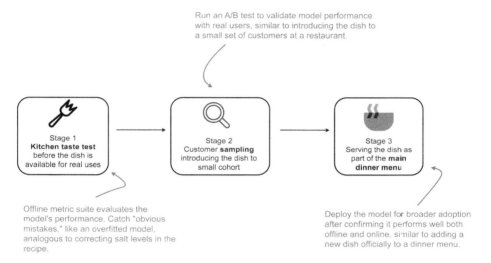

Run an A/B test to validate model performance with real users, similar to introducing the dish to a small set of customers at a restaurant.

Stage 1
Kitchen taste test
before the dish is available for real uses

Stage 2
Customer **sampling**
introducing the dish to small cohort

Stage 3
Serving the dish as part of the **main dinner menu**

Offline metric suite evaluates the model's performance. Catch "obvious mistakes," like an overfitted model, analogous to correcting salt levels in the recipe.

Deploy the model for broader adoption after confirming it performs well both offline and online, similar to adding a new dish officially to a dinner menu.

Offline evaluations generally fall into two categories: performance and diagnostics. Performance evaluations measure how well a model meets its intended objectives—common examples include metrics like accuracy, precision, recall, or ranking quality (for example, NDCG). Diagnostic evaluations, on the other hand, focus on understanding how the model behaves. These evaluations can uncover edge cases, unexpected patterns, or unintended biases that may not be visible through performance metrics alone.

To build confidence before deploying models in user-facing environments, you should rely on offline evaluations as much as possible. These evaluations help you identify the most promising model variants to move forward into A/B testing—rather than testing every possible option online. The more insights you gather up front, the less likely you are to expose users to a poorly performing model that could degrade their experience during an A/B test.

To give you an idea of what type of metrics you could tie to your offline evaluations, consider the following:

1. *Accuracy.* Calculate the proportion of correctly predicted instances out of the total predictions made on the dataset.

2. *Recall.* Measure the proportion of true positive predictions out of all positive instances in the dataset.

3. *Normalized discounted cumulative gain (NDCG).* A ranking metric that evaluates how well a list of recommended items aligns with user preferences, accounting for the order of results.

4. *Precision.* Calculate the proportion of true positive predictions out of all positive predictions made, assessing the relevance of positive predictions. The denominator, all positive predictions, include both true and false positives.

A quick caveat about offline evaluations: the metric you choose to optimize depends heavily on your use case and the maturity of your offline evaluation process. While this book focuses on online experimentation, it's worth briefly highlighting offline evaluations because they play a critical role in model development—especially when used to filter out weak variants before they ever reach an A/B test.

Let's consider recall, for example.

Recall helps you answer the question, of all the actual positive instances, how many did the model correctly identify? In the context of recommendation models on an e-commerce website, such as MarketMax, a higher recall indicates the machine learning model's ability to retrieve a larger portion of relevant items for users. This helps minimize the risk of missing important recommendations, which could negatively impact the user experience and key product metrics. Conversely, if a specific model variant has low recall, it may suggest that the model is failing to identify enough relevant items. This could suggest adjustments to the feature weights, additional training, or reevaluation of the feature set before graduating to the next step of the machine learning life cycle, the A/B testing step. Or in extreme cases, a model with persistently low recall might not graduate to online experimentation at all and is one less variant configured in your A/B test.

If you're evaluating a recommendation model that ranks items within a list, regardless of the context in which the model is used, higher values for the NDCG metric indicates a better ranking quality that could translate into positive gains in your metrics when you measure the effect in an A/B test.

Precision is particularly useful when it's crucial to ensure the relevance of positive predictions, especially in cases where false positives are costly. On the other hand, accuracy is a good metric to focus on if the cost of false positives and false negatives is essentially equal.

In general, evaluating a change in an offline setting, through offline metrics, before conducting an A/B test reduces the chance of subjecting users to less-than-ideal changes and guarantees the model's readiness for production. This proactive method of assessing machine learning's impact on a product is a responsible practice, showing dedication to the users who rely on and interact with the product.

Illustrating Benefits of Offline Evaluations

Offline evaluations allow for faster assessments of changes, such as hyperparameter tuning, feature selection, or algorithm updates, without consuming live testing resources. These evaluations are quicker to execute because they use historical or simulated datasets rather than requiring live traffic and real-time user interactions in an A/B test.

Offline evaluations also provide a safe debugging and validation environment. Testing models on historical data or in controlled conditions allows teams to analyze inputs, outputs, and potential edge cases without exposing predictions to users. Offline evaluations ensure that data pipelines, feature engineering processes, and model outputs align with expectations before deployment. Any issues, such as skewed predictions or metric inconsistencies, can be caught at this stage.

More broadly, offline evaluations can act as a risk mitigation tool, creating a controlled setting to observe the behavior of machine learning models. By evaluating performance offline, teams can confidently measure both the potential opportunities and risks associated with introducing the model variant to real users.

To maximize the benefits of offline evaluations, it's important to opt for metrics that capture both opportunities and risks of introducing a machine learning model. Metrics should measure how well the model achieves its primary objective: to improve the product experience (for example, relevance, precision, recall). They should also assess potential unintended consequences, such as fairness issues, biases, or performance bottlenecks, often referred to as diagnostic offline evaluations.

Imagine having robust offline metrics that effectively identify underperforming models before they reach the live testing stage. This can save valuable A/B testing bandwidth and time, ensuring your resources are directed toward models with the highest potential for success. Moreover, a strong offline evaluation framework strengthens your A/B testing hypotheses, making them more precise and evidence based. The better your offline evaluation platform and metrics, the more reliable your experimentation process becomes, ultimately leading to better-informed decision-making and a more impactful model deployment.

Deriving Meaning from Offline Metrics

Let's take a moment to illustrate what recall and precision look like in practice by examining a use case at MarketMax. To help customers get into the holiday spirit and ideally make purchases of craft goods, the personalization team implements a new machine learning model that recommends holiday craft goods. Before evaluating the model in a production setting through an A/B test, the team computes offline evaluations to gain initial insights into the prediction quality. More specifically, the two offline metrics that are computed in an offline setting are recall and precision.

The model achieves a recall of 80 percent. This means that the model is expected to identify 80 percent of relevant holiday craft items from the total available, with one in five relevant items potentially missed in its recommendations. In practice, this suggests that out of all relevant holiday crafts, four out of five will be successfully recommended to the user, potentially increasing engagement.

The precision for the model is 87 percent. This means that, in practice, out of all recommendations made to users, 87 percent are expected to be relevant (for example, holiday craft goods the user is interested in). Put differently, approximately one in eight recommendations might not match user interests, while seven out of eight should be relevant and potentially lead to engagement. As a reminder, precision of a machine learning model is defined by the number of true positives divided by all positives. Precision is important because if it isn't high enough, then MarketMax will serve too many irrelevant craft goods to the users.

Each metric tells a different part of the story; deciding which to focus on depends on the scenario the machine learning model is applied to.

Practicing Offline Evaluations

The idea here is to use offline evaluations as a "pre-check" to guide and refine your online experiments. By validating or filtering out lower-performing model variants in the offline stage, you can save time and resources while reducing the number of test variants in your online A/B tests, as shown in the image on page 83. Fewer test variants means smaller sample size requirements and more available testing capacity on the platform—definitely a win.

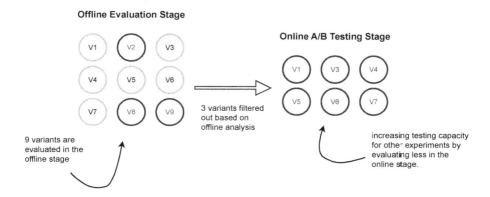

So why are we talking about offline evaluations in a book about online experimentation? Simple: a solid offline evaluation suite sets you up for success. It allows you to run better-designed, more thoughtful experiments because you've already filtered out the lower-performing candidates. This means you don't need to rely on a sizable number of test variants in your online experiments, and you'll also go into your online evaluation with a sense of how users might respond to the model's output.

With this in mind, let's see what offline and online correlation looks like in the next section.

Understanding Why Offline-Online Correlation Is Challenging

Correlating offline metrics with A/B test (online) metrics can unlock valuable insights into how changes in machine learning models impact real-world outcomes. When done well, building a solid correlation between offline and online metrics increases confidence in your offline evaluation process and can help teams make decisions earlier in the development cycle, saving time and resources. Building a correlation database between offline and online metrics will increase confidence in your offline evaluation strategy, potentially enabling teams to make more decisions based on offline evaluations.

This sounds great in theory, but offline and online metrics don't always align perfectly. To get this right, it's important to identify the offline objective that best approximates or directionally influences your online objectives. For example, offline accuracy or loss metrics might serve as a proxy for online goals like user engagement, click-through rates, or retention.

To calculate correlation, follow these high-level steps:

1. Select past A/B tests where machine learning models were evaluated.

2. For each A/B test, compute metrics that reflect user interactions and engagement with the product (online metrics).

3. Using historical data, compute offline metrics for the corresponding machine learning models.

4. Establish a mapping between the offline metrics and the online metrics from the A/B tests.

5. Analyze and visualize the relationship between these metrics. Statistical techniques, such as correlation analysis, can quantify the strength and direction of the relationship. You might use correlation coefficients, such as Pearson's correlation coefficient, to measure this relationship.

It's important to recognize that in some situations reducing the duration of an experiment isn't feasible, especially when increased confidence in insights is required or when your metrics need more time to produce meaningful results. In such cases, it may be beneficial to invest in an offline evaluation platform. Just as having a standardized approach for A/B testing is essential, prioritizing machine learning warrants the creation of a strategy for executing offline evaluations easily and at scale. This strategy should standardize the scheduling, computation of results, and aggregating results so they're accessible in the future for online correlation. This allows teams to iterate more quickly based on offline metrics that are highly correlated with online effects before moving to the more time-intensive online experimentation stage.

As stated earlier in this section, the idea of offline-online correlation is attractive, but in practice it's difficult to achieve. Let's explore why offline-online correlation isn't as easy as you'd hope.

Illustrating the Challenges

Despite the potential that's often illustrated with offline-online correlation, achieving reliable correlation is notoriously difficult. Several factors contribute to this complexity, including differences in context, mismatched objectives, and the inherent noise in online metrics.

See the cause-and-effect (fishbone) diagram on page 85 illustrating the challenges of achieving reliable offline-online correlation. Each branch represents a category of challenges, with subbranches detailing specific contributing factors.

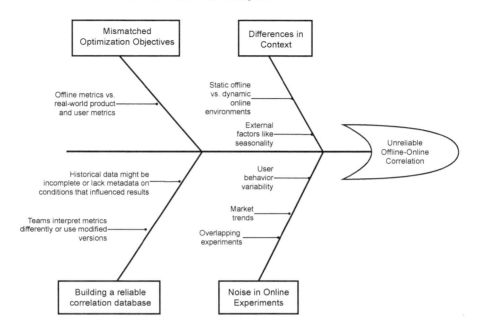

Unreliable Offline-Online Correlation
Cause-and-Effect Fishbone Diagram

As you can see from the diagram, the root causes for unreliable offline-online correlation are represented by the branches, such as contextual differences and noise in online metrics. Let's explore these factors in more detail in the next section.

Highlighting Differences in Context

Offline evaluations are conducted in controlled, static environments, typically using historical or simulated datasets. These datasets capture past user behaviors and interactions, allowing teams to test machine learning models in isolation. While this approach provides consistency and repeatability, it cannot account for the dynamic and ever-changing nature of live user environments.

In contrast, online evaluations occur in dynamic production environments where real users interact with the model. User behavior in this setting is influenced by a range of factors:

- *Seasonality.* For instance, purchasing behavior on an e-commerce site may spike during holidays or sales, making it difficult to attribute outcomes solely to model changes.

- *Promotions.* Special discounts or campaigns may artificially inflate or suppress metrics.

- *Ecosystem effects.* Changes in other features, such as a redesigned user interface or updated recommendation algorithms, can alter user engagement and confound the results.

These contextual differences make it difficult to ensure that improvements observed offline will translate to similar outcomes online. For example, a model with high offline precision might struggle to perform well online if user preferences have shifted since the dataset was collected.

Addressing Mismatched Optimization Objectives

Offline evaluations typically optimize for surrogate metrics like loss functions, ranking scores, or classification accuracy. While these are useful for fine-tuning models, they may not directly align with the ultimate online goals, such as revenue, retention, or user satisfaction.

For example, a recommendation model optimized for NDCG offline might focus heavily on ranking the most popular products at the top of the list. While this strategy might yield high scores offline, it could fail to drive meaningful user engagement online if those popular items were already well known to users. Aligning offline metrics with online objectives requires not only careful metric selection but also domain expertise to understand what truly matters to users and the business.

Understanding which offline objective directionally influences specific online outcomes requires deep domain knowledge, iterative experimentation, and a thoughtful approach to metric selection. Without this alignment, even well-optimized offline models can underperform when deployed in a live environment.

Managing Noise in Online Metrics

Online metrics obtained from A/B tests are often noisy, impacted by external factors like market trends, user variability, seasonality, or concurrent experiments. This noise can obscure the relationship between offline performance and online outcomes, making it difficult to isolate the true effects of model changes.

For instance, a model might show strong offline results but fail to deliver the expected online impact due to unrelated fluctuations in user behavior or competing changes in the product.

Building a Reliable Correlation Database

Another layer of complexity arises when attempting to systematize offline-online correlation. This involves creating a robust framework that consistently tracks, measures, and improves the relationship between offline evaluations and online outcomes. A key component of this framework is a correlation database, which serves as a centralized repository of insights across experiments, models, and metrics.

Building and maintaining such a database is a multifaceted process that requires careful consideration of the details that matter, such as a consistent schema for recording offline and online metrics and a unified metric dictionary that includes definitions, formulas, and the intended use cases for each metric.

Incorporating Offline Evaluations into Experimentation

Despite these challenges, offline evaluations remain a powerful tool for increasing the experimentation rate for machine learning models. By filtering out low-performing candidates early, teams can conserve A/B testing capacity and focus on changes with the highest potential for impact. However, it's important to recognize that no offline evaluation can fully replace the need to test in a live production setting. The production environment provides the ultimate validation of whether a model delivers meaningful value to users.

Although this chapter emphasizes offline evaluations to increase your experimentation rate for machine learning models, there will always be a need to evaluate changes in a true production setting. The more tools you have in your experimentation tool kit, the more options you have to learn and gain insights.

Next, let's explore a framework that's used in machine learning use cases in the next section.

Increasing Reward with Multi-Armed Bandits

Imagine you're at a restaurant with buffet-style dishes. Each dish has its own distinct taste profile. You didn't come to the restaurant super-hungry, so your appetite is limited, but at the same time, you want to sample as many dishes as possible while avoiding the less tasty dishes. To optimize your dining experience, you strategically sample dishes based on your past experiences and adjust to increase satisfaction in terms of eating the best-tasting dishes possible by forgoing the samples you didn't like and continuing to eat the dishes you did like. This dining experience is similar to a multi-armed bandit that aims to maximize reward while balancing exploration.

A multi-armed bandit (MAB) algorithm reframes the A/B testing problem by increasing exposure for the variant that is more optimal. An optimal solution is one that yields the highest reward, such as clicks, engagement, or revenue. At a glance, the multi-armed bandit algorithm learns the expected reward for each solution in the pool of candidates to explore and selects the optimal solution to exploit to maximize cumulative reward or gain in metrics.

With the basic understanding of multi-armed bandits top of mind, let's see how it compares to the classic A/B test.

Comparing Multi-Armed Bandits to A/B Testing

In a classic split A/B test, users are assigned to groups A and B to explore and understand the impact of each version. After the test concludes, the most successful version is typically shipped to production. The main drawbacks of the classic A/B test, particularly when compared to a multi-armed bandit approach, are twofold: first, the inferior version is usually discarded after the test, potentially overlooking valuable insights. Second, while the test is running, you may experience lost metric gains due to the inferior version being exposed to a portion of users. For example, if one variant involves an underperforming machine learning model, users assigned to that group may continue to experience a suboptimal experience for the duration of the test, which can negatively impact key metrics.

With a multi-armed bandit, after the exploration phase defines the optimal candidate, the algorithm exploits the best version to maximize reward. Users will be exposed to the winning version sooner than they would in a classic A/B test. If you find that you're running enough A/B tests oriented around evaluating machine learning models, it's worth investing engineering time toward implementing an MAB framework to reap the benefits and combat the drawbacks of traditional A/B testing. See the image on page 89.

This technique is not to be confused with multivariate experiments. Multi-armed bandits focus on real-time decision-making to optimize outcomes, whereas multivariate experiments aim to understand how different variables interact to find the best combination.

In a multivariate experiment, you're evaluating more than one variable together to understand the effect of various elements within a product experience and find out the effective combination. From an engineering platform perspective, there's a fundamental difference in the user assignment logic,

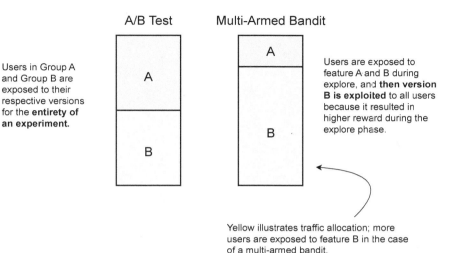

A/B Test   Multi-Armed Bandit

Users in Group A and Group B are exposed to their respective versions for the **entirety of an experiment.**

Users are exposed to feature A and B during explore, and **then version B is exploited** to all users because it resulted in higher reward during the explore phase.

Yellow illustrates traffic allocation; more users are exposed to feature B in the case of a multi-armed bandit.

where the multi-armed bandit allocates resources dynamically based on ongoing results, and the multivariate experiment has a fixed allocation across all combinations, similar to a classic split A/B test.

It's important to note that multi-armed bandits are often more effective when dealing with more dynamic environments or when there's a strong emphasis on exploration versus exploitation balance.

Next, let's delve into the fundamental concepts encompassing a multi-armed bandit.

Defining the Fundamentals of Multi-Armed Bandits

The core concepts in a multi-armed bandit algorithm are the following:

1. *Explore.* Learning the performance of each solution in the set of solutions to evaluate.

2. *Exploit.* Selecting the best option that results in the highest reward to maximize cumulative gain.

3. *Arm.* A single version that is up for evaluation within the larger candidate pool of solutions to evaluate.

4. *Reward.* Metric to optimize toward, similar to a success metric in a classic A/B test.

5. *Agent.* The system that explores and exploits.

To illustrate, see the following image.

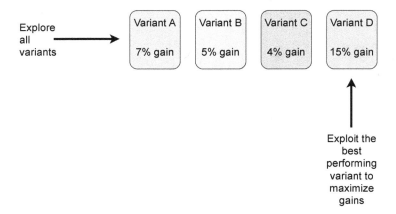

Variants A, B, C, and D are arms, also called bandits. To figure out the optimal arm, the algorithm explores X percent of the time and exploits the remaining time by pulling the best arm to increase the total reward. Based on the exploration, version D will be pulled to exploit because it's the best arm, resulting in a higher reward.

Circling back to the restaurant buffet-style experience at the beginning of this section, these same core concepts in a multi-armed bandit can be applied. See the following:

1. *Explore.* Learning each dish's performance, or taste, in the set of dishes available at the buffet.

2. *Exploit.* Selecting the best dish that results in the highest reward, taste, to maximize eating delicious food.

3. *Arm.* A single dish up for evaluation within the larger set of dishes available at the buffet.

4. *Reward.* The taste and satisfaction; some dishes will be more delicious than others.

5. *Agent.* The system that explores and exploits.

Take note of the exploration-exploitation trade-off in this buffet example. You want to explore different dishes to discover which ones are the most enjoyable, but you also want to exploit your knowledge by repeatedly selecting the dishes you know you like to maximize your dining experience. This same trade-off is present in multi-armed bandit algorithms to evaluate machine learning models on a product.

Next, let's see how you could implement a multi-armed bandit algorithm on the MarketMax website.

Illustrating Multi-Armed Bandits at MarketMax

The Ads team at MarketMax has a new banner message they want to introduce at the top of MarketMax's website to promote holiday crafts. The Ads team is evaluating four versions of the banner message, each with varying text and imagery.

If you were to evaluate each banner message in the scope of an A/B test, you would configure a test variant for each distinct banner message so it would be an A/B/C/D experiment. However, you realize this approach has two key factors that increase the cost of running such an experiment. First, you may lose engagement for the underperforming banner or test variant. Second, you may prevent other A/B tests from running on the experimentation platform because this particular test requires more users to support the four distinct test variants.

The Ads team would prefer to opt for an evaluation methodology that explores which banner message is most performant and then presents the ideal banner to users to increase reward sooner instead of waiting for insights from a traditional experiment.

In your quest to support the Ad team's main objective of maximizing engagement, through clicks on a banner, you decide to design a high-level approach for multi-armed bandits at MarketMax in your next Engineer Task.

Engineer Task: High-Level Multi-Armed Bandit Design

To apply a multi-armed bandit framework for the Advertising team's use case, you'll need to define the arms, reward, and agent.

 Engineer Task: How would you define the key components of a multi-armed bandit in the context of MarketMax?

Let's start by defining the most straightforward attribute: the arms. In the MarketMax use case, the arms would be the different versions of the message presented in the banner at the top of the website. Each arm will be exploited by the agent, and the top arm will be pulled to expose more users to increase the reward.

What did you brainstorm for the reward to optimize toward? If you were thinking of click-through rate, that metric would certainly work. Another metric that could be measured in place of click-through rate is craft good purchases attributed to the promotional message on the banner. Maximizing reward in the context of purchases is an excellent utilization of the multi-armed bandit framework because you're ideally exposing more users to the optimal solution quicker, increasing purchases more than you would in a classic A/B test.

Knowing what the reward and arms are, how did you imagine the agent would be implemented? In the simplest form, the agent could be a system or data pipeline that computes the average click-through rate attributed to each banner message sent for the previous day, then selects the message with the highest average click-through rate to exploit to maximize reward.

For more detailed information on the different multi-armed bandit solutions, check out a paper titled "Algorithms for multi-armed bandit problems" by Volodymyr Kuleshov and Doina Precup.[1]

By improving how you evaluate machine learning on your product, you're reducing the cost of innovation and also accelerating insights with more advanced strategies such as multi-armed bandits. Let's move from one algorithm to another by exploring how interleaving can be used to evaluate multiple ranking solutions in a single test variant.

Comparing Multiple Rankers with Interleaving

The most common use case for machine learning is ranking items in a list for a user to engage with. Ranking algorithms can positively impact the user experience in search, personalized home pages, advertisements, and e-commerce recommendations. Think of your most recent experience navigating a website. A ranking algorithm likely operates behind the scenes to deliver the most relevant content to you.

Given the prominence of ranking in user-facing products, it's important to enhance experimentation strategies to accelerate the process from ideation to launch. One effective strategy is interleaving, which enables you to compare multiple rankers within a single experiment variant.

In an interleaved experiment, you can compare multiple rankers within one test variant by generating a ranked list that combines results from each distinct ranker. This blended list is presented to the user, allowing you to test multiple ranking implementations in a single test variant. See the image shown on page 93.

---

1.   https://arxiv.org/abs/1402.6028

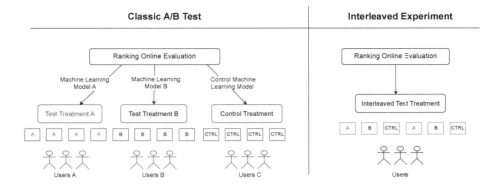

Take note of how many treatment cells there are in the classic A/B experiment versus the interleaved experiment. In an interleaved experiment, only one treatment cell incorporates all ranking algorithms into a blended list. It's important to note that this blended list is created explicitly for experimentation purposes and is shown to the user only to determine which ranker performs better.

With a basic understanding of interleaving in place, let's further explore how this strategy compares to a classic split A/B test in the following section.

Comparing Interleaving to A/B Testing

A key differentiator between a classic A/B test and an interleaved test is the metrics used to evaluate the effect. Because users are exposed to a ranked list that combines multiple rankers, you can't use metrics like weekly active users or retention, because it's challenging to correlate which ranking algorithm could have influenced those metrics. Your interleaved experiments will need metrics oriented around the content presented, such as click-through rate or engagement with the content presented to the user. Although there are restrictions with the metrics you can measure with an interleaved experiment, it's a great way to eliminate candidates and perform parameter tuning to determine the top model variants. Once the top model variants are identified, then a classic A/B test to measure metrics that are more relevant to the product but don't lend themselves well to interleaving would be employed. Revisiting the hierarchy of metrics illustrated on page 58, the metrics best suited for an interleaved experiment are at the bottom of the pyramid.

In an article written by data scientists Joshua Parks, Juliette Aurisset, and Michael Ramm, titled "Innovating Faster on Personalization Algorithms at Netflix Using Interleaving," they state:

Our second requirement was that the metrics measured in the interleaving stage need to be aligned with our traditional A/B test metrics. We now evaluate whether the interleaving preference is predictive of a ranker's performance in the subsequent A/B test.[2]

Although the metrics differ for an interleaved experiment and an A/B test, there should be a correlation between them so you can use interleaving to properly predict the optimal rankers to evaluate in the next evaluation phase, a classic A/B experiment.

Deciding When to Run an Interleaved Experiment

When to opt for an interleaved test depends on the intent of your evaluation. To make it easier to decide to use the interleaving strategy, ask yourself the following questions:

- Do you have multiple versions of the same machine learning model but with different features or configurations that you seek to evaluate?

- Do you have different machine learning models that rank items in a similar context that you want to evaluate against each other?

- Do you want to understand the effect multiple ranking algorithms have on lower-level, more sensitive metrics such as feature-level metrics and not higher-level company metrics?

If you answered yes to any of the questions, then interleaving should be considered as a strategy to evaluate ranking algorithms on a product.

Defining the Advantages of an Interleaved Experiment

Interleaving, a method for comparing ranking systems, is typically far more sensitive than a traditional A/B test, often by two orders of magnitude. One significant benefit of interleaving is its potential to decrease the number of users assigned to a test, which is particularly advantageous if testing capacity is a challenge on your experimentation platform. Additionally, interleaving can increase testing capacity on the experimentation platform, enabling more experiments to run simultaneously.

Let's delve into how interleaving can impact the availability of testing space in your upcoming Engineer Task.

---

2.   https://netflixtechblog.com/interleaving-in-online-experiments-at-netflix-a04ee392ec55

Engineer Task: Opportunities for Interleaving

How do you think interleaving could potentially influence the A/B testing step that's illustrated in the machine learning development process? In a handful of use cases MarketMax utilizes machine learning on the product, such as the Search team's algorithms to rank craft goods or the Promotions team's models that push strategic craft goods based on the time of year and seasonality. Similarly, the Marketing team relies on machine learning models for their email campaigns to drive users to visit the website for their next craft good purchase.

 Engineer Task: How can interleaving enhance the machine learning evaluation process?

Given that ranking algorithms plays a large role in selecting the right content for users on the MarketMax website, you likely realized that interleaving could increase testing capacity. Interleaving doesn't remove the need for the classic A/B test, but it does influence and inform you which candidates should graduate to the final experimentation stage in the machine learning development process.

It's best to add interleaving in between the offline evaluation stage and A/B testing. With each evaluation step, you should see the number of machine learning ranking model variants decrease as you funnel the winning candidates from each step to the next. See the following image.

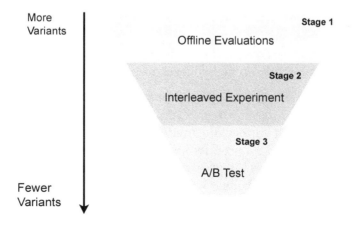

As you move from Stage 1 to Stage 3, the strategies become more focused on fewer test variants by filtering out the lower-performing candidates.

For instance, let's say you have five distinct variations of a machine learning model. Using the metrics from the offline evaluation step, you advance the top three models to the interleaving stage. Finally, after gaining insights from the interleaved experiment, you can evaluate the top two models in the final A/B testing stage.

Refer to the following image to see how these different evaluation strategies work together to assess the impact and effect of changes on your user, product, and business metrics.

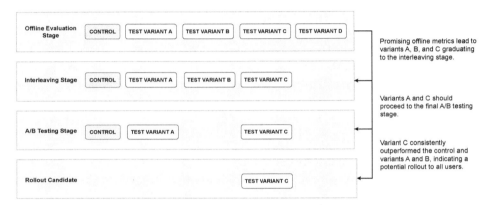

Defining the Disadvantages of an Interleaved Experiment

Interleaving also has its disadvantages. Company-level metrics such as weekly active users can't be used as a success metric, because users are exposed to multiple rankers at once, making it difficult to isolate the ranker that could have influenced a higher-level metric.

From an engineering point of view, infrastructure to support interleaving needs to scale accordingly to invoke multiple rankers within a single call. Similarly, platformizing interleaving may be difficult at a large company, given that ranking use cases on a product have differing system architectures and response time constraints. In general, the engineering logic can become complex, especially since business logic is usually intertwined with the ranker.

Now that you know both the advantages and disadvantages, let's put the interleaving strategy into practice with an example use case at MarketMax.

Illustrating Interleaving at MarketMax

Implementing the logic to enable interleaving on MarketMax's experimentation platform is tricky. The core logic to allocate users and compute metrics is the same as a traditional A/B test. However, the logic to create a blended list to present to the user that includes items from multiple rankers is custom code that you'll need to integrate into your experimentation platform.

In practice, you'll need to create an abstraction layer, in the form of a library, that captures the core interleaving logic responsible for creating the mixed list of items from multiple ranking models. The library will serve as the shared framework that engineering teams will use to fold interleaving into their system architecture. Building an interleaving library may be more challenging than it initially seems because each team can invoke a ranking model and, in general, implement a ranker differently.

Another factor to consider is the ease of use of the library. As you're incorporating this logic into the experimentation platform that's shared across the company, the library must be easy to integrate with, as it will directly influence adoption and the overhead needed to set up an interleaved test. To make interleaving a go-to solution in your experimentation tool kit, the library must scale for multiple use cases and be easy to use. With these factors in mind, let's pause to tackle your next Engineer Task in the following section.

Engineer Task: Enabling Interleaving at MarketMax

What else must the MarketMax experimentation platform team build to enable interleaving experiments on the product? You already know you need to build a core interleaving library that contains logic to invoke multiple rankers and blend the items from each ranker into a response that's reflected on the product experience. What additional piece of software do you think is missing from what's been described thus far?

 Engineer Task: What engineering frameworks are required to enable interleaving at MarketMax?

If you're wondering how teams will attribute user engagement to each ranking source, you're on the right track. Logging plays a vital role in the interleaving process. It's essential to have data that can link an item to its source algorithm. This mapping of items to sources is necessary to determine user engagement, with each ranker integrated into the final list of content displayed to the user.

Establishing a logging framework to associate served items with users and link them to specific ranking models is essential for sustainably conducting analysis. Otherwise, it will be challenging to derive which item in the blended list came from a specific ranking model. See the following image.

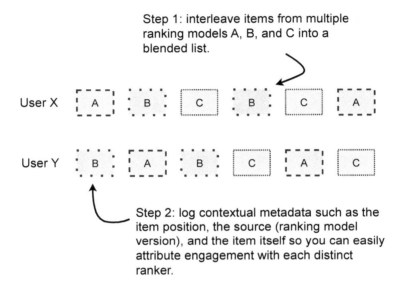

Step 1: interleave items from multiple ranking models A, B, and C into a blended list.

User X: A B C B C A

User Y: B A B C A C

Step 2: log contextual metadata such as the item position, the source (ranking model version), and the item itself so you can easily attribute engagement with each distinct ranker.

Notice how User Y and User X in the preceding image have a different ordered list of content ranked for them. The interleaving library will determine the order of the blended list of content returned to a user by invoking models A, B, and C. To attribute which ranker sourced the item served in each position to a user, you'll need a reliable logging framework to compute analysis with engagement metrics such as click-through rate.

As the MarketMax team implements the library and logging solutions to facilitate interleaving, their main focus is two key factors: performance and standardization, which are critical for optimizing the implementation.

Performance is key here because, with interleaving, you're blending results from multiple ranking models in a single request instead of calling just one model at a time like in a traditional A/B test. This added complexity can increase computation time, and if your system slows down too much, the request might time out on the front end—resulting in a poor user experience. Even if things don't time out completely, slower page load times can impact user engagement on the product, causing them to leave the page or even shift to another product.

It's well known that a slower product experience can hurt user engagement metrics, so it's especially important to monitor page load times and system response times for interleaved experiments, where there's naturally more going on behind the scenes. If you're unsure how a slower experience impacts user behavior, try running an A/B test that intentionally increases latency. This can help you understand the connection between slower load times and drops in user engagement.

Standardization is important because it creates a shared interface for blending multiple rankers into a single list and logging the right data for attribution. Having a common, reusable framework makes it much easier for teams to integrate interleaving into their workflows and simplifies debugging when things go wrong in production. Plus, a standardized approach ensures everyone is on the same page, reducing friction and saving time as more teams adopt this testing strategy.

With these new strategies to improve machine learning model evaluations in your tool kit, let's pinpoint when to implement them by reviewing the following Chapter Roundup.

Chapter Roundup: When to Implement New Strategies for Machine Learning Evaluations

Machine learning has the potential to significantly enhance business, product, and user metrics when applied appropriately within a specific context and product environment. However, if integrating machine learning into a product does not yield substantial benefits from a metrics standpoint, it's better to opt for a simpler solution. Said otherwise, don't just integrate machine learning into your product so you can say your product is machine learning driven. It's critical to measure the effectiveness of your machine learning model so you can confidently say the juice is worth the squeeze.

Additionally, it's important to recognize the potential negative impact of a poorly designed machine learning model on user engagement. For example, if a recommendation that feels irrelevant to the user is presented, they may disengage, losing trust in the product and affecting key business metrics.

Use the questions below to determine whether investing in strategies like interleaving or an offline evaluation platform is necessary to enhance your machine learning evaluation processes.

1. Are machine learning models launched to all users with poor offline metrics but gains in online metrics? If so, it may be time to revisit your offline

metrics suite and ensure you're computing metrics that can be correlated to your online test results.

2. Are broken or poor user experiences caused by machine learning A/B tests? If so, consider incorporating more offline evaluations to better inform online experiments and filter out poor performing models before a subset of users is exposed to them.

3. Are machine learning engineers frustrated with the time it takes to get insights from classic A/B tests? If so, consider implementing either interleaving or multi-armed bandits.

4. Are teams that are innovating on ranking models fighting for testing space on the experimentation platform? If so, consider implementing interleaving to increase sensitivity and evaluate ranking solutions with few users.

Answering these questions will help you decide if it's time to prioritize techniques that can accelerate and improve machine learning evaluations on your product.

Wrapping Up

Innovation and machine learning go hand in hand. Designing models that learn from user behavior to deliver better product experiences is challenging—both in terms of system design and evaluation. The slower the evaluation process, the slower your ability to innovate.

Here's a recap of the strategies and concepts covered in this chapter:

* Leverage interleaved experiments to evaluate multiple ranking solutions within a single test variant as an initial online evaluation, reducing testing capacity constraints while increasing sensitivity.

* Adopt offline evaluations to identify and filter out poorly performing models before they reach live testing, saving time and resources.

* Correlation between offline and online evaluations is the trickiest part to get right. Understanding what you're optimizing for offline—and how it nudges online outcomes—is crucial.

* Utilize metrics like accuracy, precision, recall, and NDCG to quantify model performance in offline settings and guide decision-making.

* Establish a hierarchy of evaluation strategies that balances offline evaluations, interleaving, and online A/B testing to streamline the machine learning development life cycle.

- Consider multi-armed bandit algorithms for real-time decision-making, maximizing rewards by dynamically adjusting user allocations during testing.

Now that you're well armed with new testing strategies, it's time to pivot to another core domain in advancing an experimentation platform: quality. You can run hundreds of experiments, but if the quality of insights isn't reliable or trusted, you're unlikely to make a product decision based on the test results. Rejecting hypotheses that suggest less optimal experiences is just as valuable as accepting successful hypotheses. In both instances, the quality of insights is crucial, and that's precisely what you'll explore in the next chapter.

CHAPTER 5

Verifying and Monitoring Experiments

Every product undergoes a quality check before reaching real users. Think about it: food scientists test how long a product will last on the shelf before it hits the grocery store. Video game companies rigorously test for playability and defects before releasing the game. The same principle applies to online experiments—before you start an experiment, it's really important to validate that everything's set up correctly.

In the last chapter, we focused on strategies to improve machine learning evaluations, showing how innovation in experimentation often comes from tackling the time and complexity of evaluating machine learning models. In this chapter, we're zooming out to explore frameworks for verifying an experiment before launch. These methods are universally useful—whether you're evaluating a machine learning model, a simple heuristic, or testing a brand-new UX design.

Specifically, this chapter includes the following:

- Running health checks to verify that the experimentation platform is functioning as expected.

- Incorporating verification steps into the testing process before an experiment is launched.

- Introducing a canary phase as part of the experiment ramp-up to validate variants on a small sample of users.

- Monitoring active experiments to catch issues early and ensure ongoing test quality.

Increasing experimentation capacity is great, but you know what's also great? Having a highly functional monitoring system to understand what is happening before and after an experiment launches in production.

Measuring Experimentation Effectiveness

Imagine all the ways an experiment on a product could go sideways. Maybe the test variant is misconfigured, and users never even see the new feature you're evaluating. Or maybe the control group isn't behaving like a true control, making it impossible to draw a fair comparison. Worst case? You spend days perfectly setting up the test, launch it with confidence, and then—bam!—engineering system issues pop up mid-experiment, leading to unbalanced traffic, weird sampling errors, or messy, inconclusive results.

There is good news here. You can catch many experimentation misconfigurations before they actually become an issue. With the right tools in place, you can catch issues early and make sure every experiment launched on the product is set up for success. This is especially critical as you introduce more advanced methods for evaluating a change in an online controlled setting. For instance, as you advance your experimentation platform to support interleaving and overlapping tests, it's important to complement that work with ways to monitor that everything is working as expected, given the added complexity.

The number-one goal of any experimentation platform is to enable well-designed, trustworthy experiments. A trustworthy experiment enables product decisions based on data instead of intuition or feelings. The more reliable insights are, the more knowledge your teams will have to improve user, business, and product metrics.

Before diving into the tooling that can help you verify experiments before launch and monitor active ones, let's establish the metrics you'll aim to improve. These aren't the usual product and user engagement metrics you might be used to; instead, they're platform-oriented metrics.

The goal is to monitor and demonstrate that quality is being maintained or improved as teams conduct more A/B tests over time. To achieve this, teams can track key metrics, such as the number of experiments that ended prematurely, the percentage of experiments adhering to the gold standard, the ratio of conclusive to inconclusive results, and the number of experiments that required reruns.

These metrics may reveal surprising insights. By analyzing them, you can identify trends and areas for improvement, creating insights that directly shape your A/B testing roadmap.

For example, if you notice that the number of experiments meeting the gold standard is similar to the number of experiments that ended early or inconclusive experiments, consider redefining the requirements for meeting the gold standard. This correlation should align with other metrics to some extent. If it doesn't, identifying the gaps between the gold standard and the issues leading to aborted tests or inconclusive results would be beneficial.

Some metrics, though, are bad for measuring experimentation quality. Metrics that may seem like good candidates to track but actually shouldn't be used to maintain experimentation quality are the number of product launches, number of features evaluated in the scope of an A/B test and then rolled out to all users, and number of experiments executed on the platform altogether. These metrics aren't ideal for tracking, because they could be considered in most cases a vanity metric.

A vanity metric is a data point that sounds promising, but the value proposition is unclear and can't necessarily be tied to your platform. For instance, let's say you use the number of product launches to measure the quality of your experimentation platform. If product launches in the past quarter were low, that doesn't mean you're not running high-quality experiments on your platform or that the utilization of your platform has declined.

When you're brainstorming metrics to measure the effectiveness of your experimentation practices, consider the following questions to avoid using vanity metrics:

- Can the experimentation platform team take action to influence the metric?

- Does the metric tie into the experimentation platform's strategy and vision to continue to advance experimentation practices on the product?

- Is the value proposition from the perspective of teams using the experimentation platform to run A/B tests on the product reflected by the metric definition?

- Can the metric help identify bottlenecks in the experimentation process?

- Does the metric reveal trends over time that can guide your long-term experimentation strategy?

- Does the metric encourage desirable behavior among teams that use the experimentation platform?

If you can answer yes to the preceding questions, then you have a good metric capable of tracking the quality of the experimentation platform over time.

To ensure the quality of an A/B test's configuration is met, it helps to verify before launching. Let's see what's required to verify experiments before changes to the product are exposed to a subset of users.

Verifying Experiments Before Launch

If you're an engineer, you know that you rarely, if ever, deploy a change with little validation before. For example, deploying a new version of a back-end service to production is rarely an all-at-once affair; you typically start with a canary deployment, releasing the update to a small subset of nodes to validate performance, ensure stability, and catch issues before rolling it out widely. Online controlled experiments require a similar kind of preparation and verification.

These are some of the key questions to ask before launching:

- Is the test variant working as expected?

- Is the control variant configured correctly?

- Is the overall product experience for the experiment variants meeting the basic requirements outside the scope of the new changes added?

- Is the new feature accurately rendering for the test experience and not included in the control experience?

Investing in tools and processes to verify experiments before they go live can save a lot of trouble down the road. Prelaunch verification helps teams catch and fix issues early, reducing the number of experiments that get derailed due to misconfigurations. Your goal is to start your experiment off on solid ground so it produces clean data and actionable insights.

In practice, two main approaches to prelaunch verification are used. The first is a hands-on method: validating or spot-checking specific users, like internal employees or real customers, to confirm that the test and control variants are behaving as expected. This strategy allows for quick debugging and targeted fixes when something doesn't look right.

The second approach scales things up by using programmatic systems to verify the experiment setup for a larger sample of users. This larger-scope verification strategy is ideal for detecting potential problems at scale and ensuring consistency across a broader audience.

Both methods have their strengths and are essential for building a solid prelaunch verification framework. In the sections ahead, we'll illustrate both strategies, starting with the singular user validation approach.

Building a QA Tool

You can tell a lot about what an engineering organization values by looking at how they prioritize tooling. The best engineering organizations have dedicated teams focused on building and maintaining tools, and these teams are often the unsung heroes. They're the ones engineers are endlessly grateful for, as their work consistently makes day-to-day tasks smoother, faster, and less frustrating. This may sound like an exaggeration, but it's not; well-designed tools can improve how incidents are resolved, how issues are debugged, and of course, how experiments are verified before launch.

Well-designed tools act as force multipliers, transforming complex or time-consuming tasks into streamlined workflows. They empower engineers to focus on solving high-impact problems rather than wrestling with friction in their processes. For example, tools that aid in debugging can reduce downtime and accelerate resolution during critical incidents. Monitoring tools can provide real-time insights to prevent issues before they escalate. And in the context of experimentation, robust tools can ensure that tests are verified, metrics are trustworthy, and results are actionable—ultimately reducing the time it takes to go from ideation to impact.

One tool that can make a big difference is an application designed to verify the product experience for individual users. This kind of tool is a game-changer for spot-checking tests and control variant configurations before an experiment goes live. Imagine having an internal-facing application that mirrors the product and lets you view the exact experience a specific user would see. Add in the ability to opt users into specific A/B test variants, and you've got a powerful way to catch issues before they ever reach your broader audience.

To make this tool even more effective, it should allow engineers to override contextual product details that impact the user experience, like location, device type, app version, or any other factors relevant to your product. These customizations provide flexibility and make debugging a breeze. The more details the tool can surface to help QA teams verify and debug, the better equipped your team will be to ensure test configurations are rock-solid before launch.

As an example, see the image shown on page 108 that illustrates what a MarketMax QA tool would look like.

Take a look at the right side of the QA tool in the MarketMax example—it's where an engineer or product manager can verify an experiment for a single user ID. These configurations are tailored to the MarketMax product and are

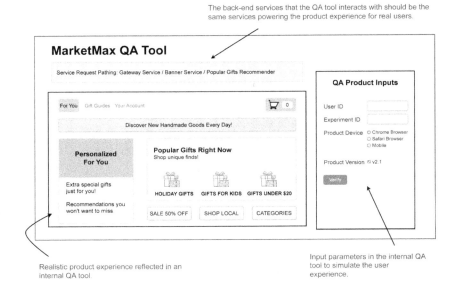

The back-end services that the QA tool interacts with should be the same services powering the product experience for real users.

Realistic product experience reflected in an internal QA tool.

Input parameters in the internal QA tool to simulate the user experience.

designed to evolve as new settings or device types are added to the product suite.

If you're building an internal QA application similar to MarketMax's, here are a few features to consider.

First, production systems are inherently complex. Adding a breadcrumb trail to your tool—one that maps out all the web services triggered as a user interacts with the product—can be a lifesaver for debugging. This feature helps you trace the flow of data step by step, making it much easier to pinpoint where things might be going wrong.

Second, this tool will likely become more than just an experiment verification tool. The closer it mimics the production experience, the more valuable it will be for debugging thorny issues or investigating customer support tickets. The effort you invest here will pay off in countless ways across your organization.

Third, QA shouldn't require assigning real users to an A/B test. Instead, your tool should let you "view" the product experience as if you were a specific user—without actually impacting the real user's experience. Think of it as a secret backdoor that allows you to explore any test or control variant to see exactly how it works, all while leaving live users untouched.

Once you've built a QA tool that mirrors the production experience, you'll find it becomes indispensable—not just for validating A/B tests but also for tackling general production issues.

That said, manual verification has its limits. A tool like this is incredibly helpful for one-off checks, but it doesn't scale well for large-scale verification. Spending hours manually inputting user IDs and checking outputs isn't practical when you need to validate configurations across hundreds or thousands of users. That's where a programmatic approach comes in. Let's explore what it takes to verify experiments at scale.

Leveraging Canaries to Catch Issues Early

To ensure more trustworthy experiments are launched in a product environment, it's valuable to adopt a programmatic approach to validating variants before fully ramping an A/B test. One effective method is incorporating a canary phase into your experimentation platform.

In practice, this involves extending the platform to include an additional step during the experiment launch process. Specifically, a small percentage of users is allocated to each variant for a brief window at the beginning of the test. This initial phase acts as a safeguard, allowing you to verify that each variant behaves as expected—without exposing the entire user base to potential issues. This canary window becomes part of the early ramp-up for a live A/B test and is often paired with a lightweight suite of validation metrics focused on system stability, logging, and metric integrity.

Once these validation checks pass, the experiment can continue ramping to larger user segments. If any issues are detected—such as a variant triggering unexpected errors, degrading key metrics, or failing to log data correctly—the rollout can be paused or halted entirely, preventing broader impact.

This approach mirrors canary deployments commonly used in back-end infrastructure and service rollouts, where a new version of a service is gradually introduced to a small subset of traffic before full deployment. Applying this concept to experimentation brings the same benefits: early detection of issues, reduced blast radius, and increased confidence in your rollout process.

As an added bonus, incorporating a canary phase into the A/B testing timeline creates a natural progression from early validation to full-scale experimentation. Once the initial metrics pass the validation suite, the canary seamlessly transitions into the broader A/B test without requiring a disruptive stop-and-start process.

In other words, this approach avoids the need to ask teams to run a short test, pause it to manually verify results, and then relaunch a full experiment—a workflow that can feel clunky and burdensome. Instead, the canary phase becomes a lightweight, integrated part of the ramp-up process. It's just another stage in the test life cycle, not a separate, disjointed task.

For teams to adopt the canary strategy consistently, the process needs to be frictionless. If validating variants feels like extra overhead, teams may skip it altogether—defeating the purpose. But if it's built directly into the experimentation workflow, is automated, and is well documented, it becomes easy to do the right thing.

Next, let's revisit MarketMax to illustrate the concept of an experimental canary.

Illustrating A/B Testing Canaries at MarketMax

At MarketMax, the team recently launched a new recommendation algorithm to improve personalized gift suggestions on the home page. Before exposing this change to a broader audience, they implemented a canary phase as part of the experiment rollout.

Using the experimentation platform, the team configured the test to allocate 1 percent of traffic to each variant—control and test—for the first two hours of the experiment. During this canary window, the platform automatically ran a validation check on system metrics, such as page load time, click-through rates, and error logs specific to the recommendation module.

This short canary phase revealed that while the new algorithm improved click-through rates, it also introduced a slight delay in loading the home page. The team used this insight to quickly roll back the test variant and refine the model before a full rollout.

By integrating the canary into the existing ramp-up process, MarketMax avoided a potentially costly user experience issue, while also building confidence in their deployment and testing workflow.

Now that you have the right tools in place to verify experiments before launch or earlier in the testing timeline, let's see what it looks like to evaluate the core infrastructure that facilitates A/B tests on the product.

Conducting Health Checks with A/A Tests

The beauty of an A/A test is that it doesn't require implementing new logic to execute. It's not a particularly flashy or groundbreaking strategy, but it's one worth emphasizing because of its practical value. By running frequent health checks with A/A tests, you can catch potential issues earlier, saving teams from spending time and resources on experiments that might yield unreliable insights.

A/A tests validate testing design and infrastructure by exposing the control and test variants to the same change. Any significant differences between two might indicate issues with data collection, experimentation infrastructure, sampling logic, or client-side instrumentation. If the A/A test shows notable differences, it suggests potential flaws in the experimental design or execution that should be resolved before running A/B tests.

The goal of an A/A test is to be as close to zero as possible on metric impact, as both variants are identical in terms of the user experience. Instead of aiming to observe a lift in metrics, you'll ideally see no difference between the test and control variants. See the following image to compare a classic A/B test to an A/A test.

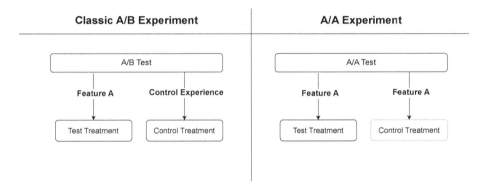

Execute an A/A test in the following scenarios: when a new feature or tool is introduced to your A/B testing platform that influences test configuration, when concerns arise regarding the quality of insights derived from an A/B test, and when there are changes such as data migrations, logging updates, or the introduction of new metrics that impact the functionality of your experimentation platform.

Next, let's explore cases where the quality of the insights gathered from an experiment should be validated for test interference and leakage.

Recognizing Spillover Effect

A spillover effect occurs when one unit's actions influence another, which can distort the results of an experiment. You'll want to avoid spillover effects, such as leakage and interference, as they can compromise the quality of your experiment's outcomes, potentially leading to incorrect decisions if left unaddressed.

Longer-term experiments are especially vulnerable to spillover effects. Let's say you're running a long-term holdback that lasts for months—users might start noticing that others have access to a new feature while they don't. That little bit of "feature envy" can change how they behave, like using the product less or differently than they normally would. When that happens, it introduces bias and makes it harder to get clean, reliable test results.

Longer experiments have many benefits. For instance, cumulative and degradation holdbacks enable you to measure the effect of a feature on a less-sensitive metric like retention. However, there's also a cost, which we'll discuss further in Chapter 8, Measuring Long-Term Impact, on page 157. For now, keep in mind that the spillover effect is one downside to long-term experiments that impacts the testing quality and insights.

Spillover effects can be especially tricky on social network platforms, where one user's actions can influence another's behavior. Imagine this: User A is in the test group, and a new feature encourages them to send more messages. Meanwhile, User B, who's in the control group, is socially connected to User A. User A's increased activity might prompt User B to engage more, even though they didn't get the new feature—contaminating the control group and messing up your results.

To avoid this, one common strategy is to cluster users into groups where no social connections exist between the test and control variants. In other words, User A and User B wouldn't be split across groups—they'd either both be in the test group or both in the control group. This approach helps isolate the effect of the experiment. On top of that, it's important to keep an eye out for any unexpected connections or biases during the experiment to make sure the groups remain clean and independent.

For more details on test spillage and social network platforms, check out the article titled "AB-Testing Challenges in Social Networks."[1]

Next, let's tie the tooling and techniques that can improve quality of experiments executed on a product by discussing how to fold in these strategies into the experimentation process.

---

1.   https://medium.com/data-science/ab-testing-challenges-in-social-networks-e67611c92916

Structuring the Experimentation Process

Now that you have the tools and strategies to ensure teams are running quality experiments, it's the perfect time to figure out how you'll introduce them into the end-to-end testing process. Without the right process, teams are unlikely to do the extra steps needed to verify experimentation configuration. But with the right process that makes it easy to fold in these strategies, your experiment quality will surely improve with ideally little effort from the teams that leverage the experimentation platform.

The three elements needed to introduce improvements to your experiment practices are strategy, tooling and infrastructure, and process.

Throughout this chapter, we've addressed strategy and tooling with concepts such as QA tooling for single use case verification and experiment canaries to verify early in the ramp-up stage. Now it's the perfect time to figure out how you'll introduce these tools into the end-to-end testing process.

Without an organized process, running experiments on a product becomes chaotic, especially once you get to the scale where multiple teams and product organizations evaluate changes simultaneously. How you structure your experimentation process around proper verification and monitoring applications directly influences the tooling's effectiveness.

Let's incorporate each strategy into the testing process, starting with the tools that you can use before a test is enabled.

Incorporating Proper Experimentation Verification

You can include verification tools as prerequisites that must be utilized before launching an experiment. For example, before an A/B test can proceed to launch, the team that owns the experiment needs to perform several validations. First, they must confirm that both the test and control variants are accurately configured by cross-referencing with employee user IDs and real user IDs, using an internal QA tool that mirrors the product experience. Following this, they'll monitor and verify experiment setup during the canary phase as part of the experiment ramp-up to validate variants on a small sample of users.

As long as your tools are easy to use and require little support from the platform team, incentivizing teams to use them should be easy. It's in the product and engineering teams' best interest to verify experiments before launching so that they don't waste time deploying a misconfigured test. Check out the image shown on page 114.

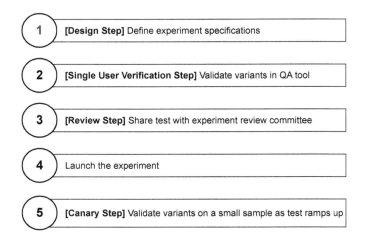

For each of these steps, the more tooling in place, the easier it will be. Steps two and three are necessary to verify the A/B test is configured correctly so you can increase confidence in your test configuration before launch. The experimentation review committee will review the simulation report as part of their review process before deeming an experiment ready for production. Similarly, the review committee should use the gold standard experiment definition to ensure the test configuration meets those requirements.

Monitoring Active Experiments Effectively

Keeping an eye on active experiments is equally important to verifying an experiment before it's launched. The only thing worse than not running an online controlled experiment to evaluate changes in your product is running an experiment that is misconfigured for weeks and weeks, resulting in inconclusive insights. This is why a key component of experimenting reliably on a product is monitoring active tests and checking for degradation and issues earlier rather than later. There's always the chance a misconfigured test is launched, but if you monitor active experiments, you'll at least catch problems earlier in the duration of a test.

To create a sustainable means for monitoring active experiments, your strategy should include the following two steps: first, an automated process that instantiates monitoring of an experiment once it has started—there should be no manual steps to kickstart the monitoring process—and second, alerting infrastructure to catch degradations in place of requiring a human to check every day.

Minimizing the need for human intervention in experiment monitoring is crucial. In deadline-driven environments, where experiments must meet specific timelines, one of the worst scenarios is discovering late in the experiment's duration that the configuration has a technical or statistical issue, forcing a restart. The more automated monitoring you have in place, the quicker you can catch issues or performance degradations, preventing high-stress situations where critical-feature launch timelines are delayed.

Like monitoring the core software responsible for orchestrating A/B testing on the product, monitoring active experiments should hold the same weight and priority. By making monitoring a priority on your roadmap, you're also protecting the user experience from malformed or invalid changes that could be potentially undesirable from a product, business, and user perspective. You also ensure that experiments are actively monitored for issues that could jeopardize the accuracy of the results, such as more significant engineering outages that result in data that cannot be used for analysis.

When implementing a strategy for monitoring active experiments, you'll need to do the following:

1. Implement alerts and logging to keep track of critical metrics. You may have to consider sampling logs in an effort to reduce the cost of storing more data if your metrics for monitoring an experiment don't exist.

2. Establish a threshold for each metric that determines what is considered a degradation and should trigger an alert.

3. Create a process to act on those alerts, communicate to stakeholders, and terminate an experiment. Building logic that can tie in experiment alerts to the team that owns the experiment so that their on-call pager is notified creates a clearer line of ownership and responsibility. The experimentation platform team owns the alerting logic and infrastructure, and the team that created the experiment owns taking action on any alerts related to their A/B tests.

You've done a fantastic job navigating all the strategies that improve experimentation quality. Take a look at the checklist in the following Chapter Roundup, which captures the techniques discussed throughout the chapter. When experimentation quality is a priority for advancing your platform, this checklist can be used to create the roadmap.

Chapter Roundup: Checklist for Creating an Experimentation Quality Roadmap

Prioritizing quality is an investment that all experimentation platform teams should make. If you lack testing standards and means for ensuring quality tests, you're more likely to waste time running misconfigured A/B tests. Use the following checklist to create a platform strategy for improving experimentation quality on a product.

1. Define the requirements to create a gold standard for running experiments on the platform. Remember that the gold standard should align with your testing best practices.

2. Create metrics that you can use to monitor experimentation quality and track whether improvements are made or degradation occurs in your experimentation platform team's goal for enabling trustworthy experiments on the product.

3. Implement verification tools, such as a QA application to spot-check users.

4. Build methods for monitoring active experiments, including checking for test leakage and interference.

5. Update your experimentation playbook to include the verification and monitoring tactics so teams are aware of the tooling available.

6. Run A/A tests periodically as a health check for your experimentation platform. They're an effective way for platform teams to ensure their infrastructure and systems are functioning correctly. A/A tests are equally valuable for product engineering teams, helping them validate their specific experimentation practices and build confidence in their setups.

Once you've tackled the preceding list, make sure to actively monitor and summarize your experimentation quality metrics so you can showcase that your strategy has been effective. These platform quality metrics will also enable you to make data-informed decisions regarding your engineering roadmap as you evolve your experimentation platform.

Wrapping Up

A/B testing is a powerful methodology, but it can also be resource intensive. To optimize the process and build trust in your results, it's crucial to verify experiment setups and actively monitor tests for quality and accuracy. These practices ensure reliable insights and help deliver the right product experiences to your users.

This chapter highlighted key strategies to improve experimentation quality, including the following:

- Verifying experiments in non-production settings before launching to users. By addressing potential configuration issues early, you minimize the risk of introducing errors or biases into live environments.

- Building internal tools to spot-check individual user experiences without impacting live settings. In top-tier engineering organizations, tooling isn't an afterthought, but rather it's a strategic investment, especially for experimentation.

- Developing scalable solutions like experiment canaries to verify configuration early in the A/B test duration.

- Running A/A tests to validate experimentation platform infrastructure and detect hidden issues. This helps ensure that the engineering systems function as intended.

- Establishing automated monitoring systems to identify and address issues in active experiments. Real-time alerts allow teams to catch issues proactively, minimizing the impact of errors on user experience and experimental results.

- Integrating verification and monitoring steps into the experimentation process to streamline workflows.

Now that you're armed with monitoring and verification tactics to improve experimentation quality, let's explore what it looks like to increase the quality of test insights.

CHAPTER 6

Ensuring Trustworthy Insights

Think back to the last time you were interviewed for a job. Every email, every conversation, and every question asked was a data point you used to learn more about the company culture. With the finite time you had during the interview process, you wanted to make the best decision you could for your career with the information you had.

The same can be said for A/B testing—with the finite time a feature is exposed to a subset of users, you want to gain as much insight, using as many data points and signals as possible, to make the right decision to evolve your product.

As you're evaluating changes in the scope of an experiment, you're keeping an eye on the quality of the experiment from a configuration perspective, as discussed in Chapter 5, Verifying and Monitoring Experiments, on page 103. You've implemented strategies to verify experiment configurations before launch and created tools to spot-check the product experience for users, so you have increased confidence in the test setup.

Quality goes beyond just the experiment configuration. It also includes how much you learn from each A/B test, whether the results are statistically valid, and the overall strength of the insights gained.

In this chapter, we'll detail strategies that increase trust and insights from running online controlled experiments on a product. Topics we'll explore include the following:

- How to replicate experiments or extend their duration to confirm findings and reduce uncertainty.

- How to reduce false positives and false negatives.

- How to aggregate data from multiple tests using meta-analysis.

Let's get into it.

Why Insights Quality Matters

Insights quality falls into two key categories: methods to increase trust and methods to increase learnings.

When you're running well-designed experiments to make product decisions, sometimes those decisions lead to launching a change to all users, and other times those decisions lead to running more experiments so the team can learn more about the impact of their product ideas.

A mix of methods is needed to advance your experimentation practices, but a clear theme in every chapter is the need for tooling. Utilizing quality-focused tools that verify test setup allows you to answer questions such as "Is the experiment configured accurately to gauge the impact of changes on the product?" and "Will the experiment guide the team toward insights capable of determining whether the feature should be rolled out to all users?"

You've already gained tactics that increased confidence in your experiment setup. Now, in this chapter, we're focusing on the quality of data insights and quality of test configuration from a statistical perspective, assuming your test setup is accurate. More specifically, we're asking, "How much can you learn from each test?" and "How trustworthy are the insights that are derived from each test?"

With these two questions in mind, we've split experimentation insights quality into two categories. See the following image.

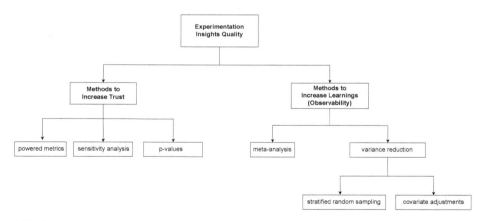

We'll discuss the methods that can improve each category throughout this chapter.

You can have a fully functioning experimentation platform, but if the design or test configuration itself isn't likely to lead to trustworthy insights, then using the data to make decisions is probably not a good idea. You wouldn't want to base product decisions on faulty or invalid experiments.

If teams often find themselves reviewing results that are inactionable, it's worth revisiting testing setup best practices that influence insights, such as the gold standard guidelines. If teams frequently replicate and rerun experiments due to initial tests being underpowered and resulting in exaggerated treatment effects, it's important to review the configuration of these experiments. Identifying which aspects need adjustment can help address the issue.

On the other hand, if you're running trustworthy experiments but not fully exploring the data, you might be missing opportunities for deeper learning. Experimentation is fundamentally about discovering what worked and what didn't. By incorporating supplementary tactics to extract more insights, teams can learn even more from each experiment.

When teams struggle to act on experiment results, it's often a sign that testing practices need a closer look. Here are a few key indicators that improvements are needed:

- Teams frequently question if external factors or biases are influencing experiment results.

- Data scientists express concerns about uncertainty in the treatment effect.

- Engineers struggle to measure the impact of changes on specific user cohorts.

- Product managers doubt the reliability of results showing small treatment effects.

- UX designers find it difficult to link experiment insights to user behavior, making it challenging to refine designs or validate hypotheses.

Keep these indicators in mind as you explore the tactics outlined in this chapter to boost insights from an A/B test.

Understanding False Positives and False Negatives

To set the stage for this chapter, it's worth emphasizing common terminology to describe experiment outcomes. In A/B testing, understanding false positives, false negatives, true positives, and true negatives is critical for interpreting results accurately and making informed decisions. These terms represent the possible results when comparing the reality of an effect (or lack thereof) to the interpretation derived from the test.

A true positive is exactly what you would expect: your new feature improves user engagement, and the A/B test correctly identifies this improvement. A true negative is when you do not detect a significant effect, and there is indeed no effect. For example, your new feature has no impact, and the A/B test correctly finds no difference. The outcome is not introducing the new feature to all users of the product. These two scenarios are your ideal outcomes; they indicate that your testing setup and analysis are working as intended.

Let's talk about less-than-ideal outcomes. A false positive is when you observe a statistically significant improvement (like a metric gain), but in reality, there isn't one. For example, your test falsely concludes that a feature improves user engagement due to random noise. Second, a false negative is when you do not detect a significant effect, but there is one. The outcome in this situation could look like a scenario where you decide not to launch a new feature, which turns out to be a missed opportunity, given it actually does improve key metrics.

To better visualize these experiment outcomes, see the table shown on page 123 illustrating a confusion matrix tailored to A/B testing. A confusion matrix is a tool used in statistics and machine learning to classify outcomes based on predictions versus reality. In the context of A/B testing, it can help break down the four possible scenarios and can serve as a reminder of what you're aiming for: an experiment design that minimizes errors while maximizing actionable insight.

True positives and true negatives are the goal. They indicate your experimentation setup and statistical analysis are working as intended.

You want to minimize false positives, also called Type I errors, because a false positive can lead to deploying a feature that doesn't benefit users, wasting resources and possibly harming the product experience. Similarly, you want to minimize false negatives, also referred to as Type II errors, because you might miss rolling out a beneficial change, slowing down innovation.

It's evident by now that A/B testing doesn't always give you clear answers. Individual tests can be noisy, and their results might not tell the full story. That's where meta-analysis comes in—it helps you look at the bigger picture by pooling insights from multiple experiments, making it easier to understand how your features are actually performing.

Actual Effect	Detected Effect	Outcome	Explanation
Effect Present	Effect Detected	True Positive	Your test correctly identifies a positive impact from your new feature.
Effect Present	No Effect Detected	False Negative	Your test fails to detect an actual positive impact, leading to missed potential.
No Effect Present	Effect Detected	False Positive	Your test incorrectly identifies an effect due to random noise or error.
No Effect Present	No Effect Detected	True Negative	Your test correctly identifies no impact.

Comparing Effect with Meta-Analysis

Imagine you're purchasing a new piece of furniture, and you want to make an informed decision. You're considering several factors, including price, size, and color. You're also considering the reviews by other people who purchased the same piece of furniture and aggregating reviews from multiple online retailers and social media platforms. As you incorporate each review into your decision framework, you're also weighting them, giving more weight to reviews from trusted online retailers. This same concept of aggregating information from multiple sources to make a more informed decision is applied to evaluating experiments on a product.

Meta-analysis is a statistical technique that can help you synthesize evidence from multiple experiments by combining data insights to gather an overall estimate of the impact of a change on a product. In simple terms, this means looking at the results from different experiments together to draw broader conclusions, increasing the reliability and generalizability of the findings.

Consider implementing meta-analysis when you want to increase statistical power by defining the combined p-value or when you aim to gain better insights by learning from experiments in aggregate. By pooling data from multiple experiments, meta-analysis can provide a more comprehensive understanding of the effect size.

Meta-analysis is also a practice carried out in the medical industry when multiple independent studies, such as clinical trials, are conducted at various medical institutions. In some cases, the study suggests the positive effects of a treatment, and in other cases, it demonstrates the negative effects. As a result, there isn't a clear consensus on the treatment effect requiring a more comprehensive analysis by combining results from multiple experiments. Examining whether the effect of a change is consistent across different experiments by combining results from multiple experiments, you'll be able to increase confidence in determining the impact of a treatment. See the paper titled "Meta-analysis in clinical trials" that can be used as inspiration for conducting similar practice on user-facing products.[1]

Now that you know what meta-analysis is at a high-level, let's revisit your role at MarketMax by tackling your next Engineer Task.

Engineer Task: High-Level Requirements for Meta-Analysis at MarketMax

Teams at MarketMax run experiments often, but they haven't built the habit of comparing insights from similar tests. They have infrastructure in place to do so, but they lack the framework, which is exactly what you'll be brainstorming in your next Engineer Task. What do you think the team needs in order to introduce meta-analysis as a technique that teams can tap into when comparing experiments and determining the effect of a treatment?

 Engineer Task: What type of data is required to implement meta-analysis?

In theory, meta-analysis consists of comparing results from multiple experiments to define a more precise estimate of impact. In practice, a mechanism to capture metadata or tags to define similar experiments is the first step before conducting the analysis. Teams need an easy way to group experiments that evaluate similar features and related changes on the product to compare the right experiments to each other. The experiments could be organized by product themes or use cases.

Meta-analysis works by bringing together a few key pieces of information. First, it relies on results from multiple related experiments to identify patterns that a single test might not reveal. Keep in mind two keywords in that prior

---

1.   https://pubmed.ncbi.nlm.nih.gov/3802833/

sentence: related experiments. To understand if experiments are related, you'll also need metadata to draw those conclusions, such as the hypotheses tested and how the experiments are categorized, to provide context and help interpret the combined results accurately. And lastly, you'll need key details about how each experiment was set up, like sample sizes and statistical thresholds, to ensure the analysis is sound.

As you compare data insights, you're also giving each experiment a weight based on factors related to the experimentation configuration. For example, experiments with larger sample sizes are given more weight than those with smaller ones. At MarketMax, teams use the hierarchy of tests illustrated on page 64. For experiments that are classified as *test to learn*, the duration is short compared to a *test-to-measure* experiment. In that case, a test-to-learn experiment would have less weight than a test to measure when conducting meta-analysis.

Meta-analysis should only be performed when multiple experiments address the same or very similar questions; if they differ, the measurements from each test aren't really worthy of comparison to each other.

Just as running A/A tests periodically helps ensure the quality of your experimentation platform, incorporating meta-analysis into your quarterly or yearly review process can provide valuable insights into the overall effectiveness and consistency of your experiments.

Combating Errors with Meta-Analysis

Meta-analysis is a valuable tool for experimentation that can help you make better decisions by looking at data across multiple tests. Instead of treating each experiment in isolation, meta-analysis allows you to combine results to get a clearer understanding of how your features are performing overall.

Experimentation is rarely perfect—errors happen. Sometimes you'll see false positives, where an experiment seems to show a positive impact, but in reality, there's no meaningful difference between the test and control groups. Other times, you might encounter false negatives, where a test fails to show an improvement, even though there's actually something there.

By pooling data from multiple experiments, meta-analysis helps cut through the noise. It can reveal trends that individual tests might miss, giving you a better sense of the real impact your changes have on the product and user experience. It's not about eliminating uncertainty entirely—that's impossible—but rather about stacking the odds in your favor to make more informed, reliable decisions.

Building Product Intuition with Meta-Analysis

An often-overlooked detail is the importance of having strong product intuition. The more you know about your metrics, how users use the product, and how changes impact key metrics, the more informed your testing strategy will be. If you're evaluating changes with the wrong metrics, you're wasting time and critical testing capacity on the product.

Meta-analysis is a great method for building intuition as to what type of impact to expect from a feature based on past experiments. If you've executed an A/B test on a product, you should have an understanding of why a feature tanked a particular metric and recognize where things are going against patterns that have been observed by past experiments.

Building strong product intuition doesn't mean you'll always be right, but it is critical to catching false positives early and questioning when test results are invalid.

Considering Metric Sensitivity in Relation to Quality Insights

Let's say you're optimizing a biscotti recipe and want to assess how different amounts of almonds affect the final taste. While evaluating different variations of almond quantity, you're analyzing the difference in the biscotti flavor for each variant while keeping other ingredients consistent. From this study, you determine that adding slightly more almonds gives the biscotti a much more intense nutty taste profile. This process is similar to sensitivity analysis in A/B testing, where you assess how small a change can be detected in a metric.

The more sensitive a metric is, the better it is for detecting changes in an experiment. The less sensitive a metric is, the harder it will be to detect an effect, leading to smaller treatment effects or unclear conclusions. In other words, if you can increase metric sensitivity, then you increase the chance of detecting small changes, which is valuable when evaluating features on a product. If you can't attain the sensitivity that matters for your product, it's typically a result of selecting high-variance metrics in which you should consider selecting better metrics to evaluate experiments with.

One way to increase sensitivity is to increase the sample size in your experiment configuration. Although this is the simplest option, it's not always ideal in situations where many teams are fighting for the same testing space or if testing availability is a constraint. Another way to increase sensitivity is through variance reduction strategies, which we'll explore next.

Increasing Precision with Stratified Random Sampling

Stratified random sampling is a variance reduction method used to increase precision in the insights from an experiment, thereby improving insight quality. Variance reduction refers to incorporating techniques that minimize the variability in the observed outcome. By reducing variance, you increase the sensitivity of your experiment, which improves the likelihood of detecting the true effect of the changes being evaluated.

Stratified random sampling is one type of variance reduction strategy. The benefits of incorporating such into your experimentation practice include increased sensitivity so you can detect true treatment effects within your experiment, improved precision by calculating effects within subgroups that may be created based on attributes that could influence the measured outcome, and richer analysis that can lead to meaningful insights into the effect of changes on specific user groups.

Stratified random sampling can be applied in the context of A/B testing to control for potential sources of variation and improve the accuracy of comparisons between the treatment and control groups. See the following image for a high-level illustration of strata (distinct subgroups within a population defined by shared attributes, such as demographics) that can be used to derive treatment effects.

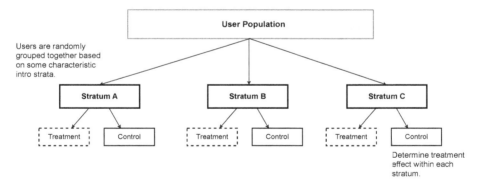

Let's break down how stratified random sampling might work on a platform like MarketMax. Imagine you're running an experiment to evaluate a new recommendation algorithm.

The first step is to identify meaningful strata—distinct subgroups within your user base that share common attributes likely to influence the outcome. Start by analyzing your user base to determine which attributes significantly impact the metrics you care about. For MarketMax, these attributes might include the following:

- *Purchase frequency.* Monthly active buyers vs. yearly active buyers.
- *User tenure.* New users vs. returning users.
- *Geographic region.* Users from North America, Europe, or Asia.
- *Device type.* Mobile vs. desktop users.

It's a good idea to work with data scientists who are familiar with user behavior on the product to prioritize attributes that are most likely to impact the experiment's outcome.

The second step is to divide the user population into these strata based on the identified attributes, such as these:

- *Stratum 1.* Monthly active buyers using mobile devices.
- *Stratum 2.* Yearly active buyers using desktop devices.

Once the strata are defined, ensure that users are randomly assigned within each subgroup to the test or control variant. This step ensures balance and preserves the diversity of your population while controlling for key differences.

The third key step is to analyze the subgroup-specific effects by calculating the metric for each subgroup separately. For example, you might discover that the new recommendation algorithm significantly improves conversion rates for monthly active buyers but has little impact on yearly active buyers.

Finally, after analyzing each stratum, aggregate the results to understand the overall impact of the experiment. Use weighted averages based on the size of each stratum to calculate the combined treatment effect. For instance, if monthly active buyers account for 70 percent of your user base, their results should carry more weight in the overall estimate.

Illustrating Benefits of Stratified Random Sampling

As a variance reduction strategy, stratified random sampling comes with three key benefits: increased sensitivity, improved precision, and richer insights. By reducing noise, it makes it easier to detect true treatment effects, boosting sensitivity. This strategy also improves precision by allowing you to measure effects within specific user cohorts. Most importantly, stratified random sampling helps uncover meaningful insights about how changes impact different user groups—revealing trends that might otherwise fly under the radar.

While stratified random sampling offers significant advantages, it's important to carefully select attributes that meaningfully segment your population without overcomplicating the analysis. Too many strata can lead to small sample sizes within each group, reducing statistical power. Focus on a handful of attributes that are most relevant to the experiment's goals.

Reducing Variance with Stratified Experiments

Your experimentation design directly influences the quality of the insights you'll gain from the online controlled experiment. The better your experiment design is, the stronger your insights will be to make decisions from. As you implement stratified random sampling into your experimentation platform, teams may wonder why they should opt for this strategy over a test that leverages randomized sampling. The main implication from choosing a randomized experiment versus a stratified experiment is the variance.

Variance plays a critical role in experiment design because it determines how easily you can detect statistically significant differences between the control and test variants. A higher variance makes it harder to identify these differences, requiring larger sample sizes or longer test durations to achieve reliable results. Conversely, a lower variance makes it easier to detect meaningful differences, reducing the resources and time required to reach conclusive insights. This is where stratified experiments shine.

Stratified experiments are an effective variance reduction technique that can improve the sensitivity of your experiment design. By dividing the user population into subgroups, or strata, based on key characteristics that are good predictors of the potential outcome, you can ensure that the variability within each group is minimized. For example, if you're running an experiment on an e-commerce platform, stratifying users by geographic region, purchase history, or device type might reduce variance because these factors often influence user behavior. By analyzing the results within these more homogeneous strata, you gain a clearer picture of how the tested change affects different segments of your user base.

While stratified random sampling is a powerful technique, it's just one of many strategies available to reduce variance and increase sensitivity in experiment design. Understanding when to use this approach and how to complement it with other techniques is critical to building a robust experimentation framework.

Let's look at another variance reduction strategy that can increase sensitivity and improve the quality of insights gathered from an experiment.

Measuring Outcomes with Covariate Adjustments

The covariate adjustment strategy can lead you to more accurate estimates in online controlled experiments. The word *covariate* can be translated into variables that could influence the outcome of a test, such as user demographics or a user's historical usage behaviors. And the word *adjustments* can be translated to a statistical model that considers the covariates. By adjusting for covariates, the model can control for their influence, leading to more precise insights from the experiment results.

The high-level steps to introduce covariate adjustments into your experimentation platform are the following:

1. Identify covariates that may influence an experiment's outcome or measured effect.

2. Ensure covariates are randomly distributed in the test and control variants without any imbalances.

3. Implement a statistical model, such as linear or logistic regression, with covariates as independent variables to account for the adjustments.

4. Perform the adjustments for the covariates.

5. Estimate treatment effects.

6. Interpret the covariate-adjusted treatment effect.

Now that you have a general idea of the tactics that can increase sensitivity and improve insights from each experiment, let's see what it looks like to ensure those insights are trustworthy.

Navigating False Positive Risk

When engineering and product organizations get into the swing of using this evaluation methodology on the product, test results feel like a gift you anticipated for weeks, unsure of what could be inside—metric gains or metric degradation. Before ordering the celebratory cake when an experiment suggests positive gains in metrics, it's essential to verify the experiment insights are accurate to avoid false positives.

A false positive occurs when you mistakenly conclude that a test variant had an impact, but in actuality, any observed difference is caused by random variability. In practice, this impacts your decision because you're basing the decision on an understanding that the treatment had a meaningful effect. To increase trust in your experimentation insights and quality, you want to reduce the probability that a statistically significant result is a false positive.

It's important to minimize false positives in experimentation because they can lead to significant consequences, including these:

- Steering the product roadmap in the wrong direction, wasting resources on ideas that don't deliver real value.

- Rolling out new features to all users that fail to improve the user experience as expected based on misleading experiment results.

- Experiencing unexpected metric degradation when the change is launched at scale, as the supposed gains observed during the experiment don't hold up.

Replicating Experiments

The most straightforward method for reducing the risk of false positives is replicating the experiment. As you review test results, you can establish organizational guidelines that define when a repeat experiment is necessary. For example, if the p-value score is small, repeat the experiment with higher power. Establishing organizational guidelines that define when replication is necessary can help standardize this practice. For example, a guideline might recommend replication if the p-value score is significant but close to the threshold (for instance, 0.04) or if the observed effect size deviates significantly from historical norms.

When replicating experiments, consider adjusting the experiment design to improve its rigor. For instance, if the initial test included multiple test variants, simplifying the setup by focusing on a single variant compared to the control can help achieve higher statistical power and reduce variability. This approach allows you to allocate more users to the critical comparison, increasing the likelihood of detecting true effects while minimizing noise.

Repeating an experiment also provides an opportunity to address any potential flaws or uncertainties in the original experiment setup. Were the metrics sensitive enough to detect changes? Was the randomization process robust? By addressing these questions during replication, you can refine your methodology and further reduce the risk of false positives.

Another advantage of replication is its role in building organizational trust. Teams and stakeholders are more likely to act on experiment results when they know those findings have been confirmed through repeat testing. This is particularly valuable when the stakes are high, such as launching a major product change or making decisions with long-term implications.

The second simplest method for reducing the false positive risk is to run your experiment longer.

Running Experiments Longer

Extending the duration of your experiment can be a useful strategy to reduce the likelihood of a false positive. Keep in mind that the running the experiment for a longer duration is not intended to allocate more users to each variant but rather provide additional data from existing users already allocated to the variants, which may help improve confidence in detecting true effects.

While extending the duration is a relatively low-cost method to improve test quality, it does require careful consideration of diminishing returns. The benefit of additional data diminishes over time as the experiment approaches the point of statistical saturation, where adding more observations no longer significantly improves confidence. Monitoring metrics like confidence intervals or p-value stabilization can help you decide when the experiment has run long enough.

If you're not constrained by time, running experiments longer can be a relatively low-cost way to improve the quality of your test results. This approach is particularly beneficial in cases where the metric of interest has high variability or when the sample size in each variant is relatively small.

Doubling Down on Statistical Power

Running trustworthy experiments should always be the goal of your experimentation platform because you're making decisions based on the outcomes from experiments that influence metrics, user experience, and product roadmap. You were introduced to statistical power in Chapter 3, Designing Better Experiments, on page 51, as it's highly coupled to the success and guardrail metrics selected for an experiment's configuration. In this section, we'll emphasize the importance of powering your experiments so that A/B tests executed on the platform result in trustworthy insights.

As a reminder, statistical power is the ability to detect a meaningful difference between the experiment's variants when there is one and rejecting the null when there's a true difference in the minimal detectable effect (MDE). The higher your statistical power is for an experiment, the more likely you'll be able to identify the true effect. You reduce the likelihood of detecting the true effect if you've configured an underpowered test. Small improvements in metrics like revenue can add up significantly over thousands of experiments each year, which makes small effects valuable in this context.

In situations where most of your experiments are coming back inconclusive, you're likely lacking enough statistical power to detect the changes evaluated in each experiment. Now if you do have enough statistical power and your metrics are flat or neutral, then you've learned that your changes aren't moving metrics as you likely hoped for.

Even large companies with millions of users face low statistical power when detecting small but meaningful effects. In practice, it's difficult to power experiments sufficiently as the demand for experimenting on the product increases. If your experimentation platform has the capacity and you're questioning the results of an experiment that was underpowered, you should consider rerunning the experiment with a larger sample size. While a larger sample size can improve sensitivity, this approach has clear limitations and doesn't necessarily guarantee statistical significance. Refer back to Chapter 3, Designing Better Experiments, on page 51, particularly the section on the capping metrics technique, to further improve statistical power.

Preventing False Positives and False Negatives

Before we wrap up this chapter, let's take a moment to revisit the two main categories of experimentation-insights quality we discussed: increasing trust and deepening learnings. The tactics you've explored throughout this chapter aim to improve the reliability of A/B test results while helping you minimize common errors like false positives and false negatives. The image shown on page 134, which you saw earlier, now includes added context about how these strategies relate to reducing your chances of a false negative or false positive error.

When it comes to preventing false positives, key strategies include using p-values, meta-analysis, and variance reduction techniques. Properly inter-preting and calibrating p-values ensures statistical thresholds are met, lowering the chances of incorrectly declaring an effect where none exists. Aggregating data from multiple experiments through meta-analysis can validate insights and filter out random noise. Variance reduction techniques, such as stratified random sampling and covariate adjustments, further reduce noise in the data, making your results more accurate.

To tackle false negatives, strategies like sensitivity analysis, ensuring properly powered metrics, and applying variance reduction techniques are essential. Sensitivity analysis can help you spot subtle but meaningful effects that might

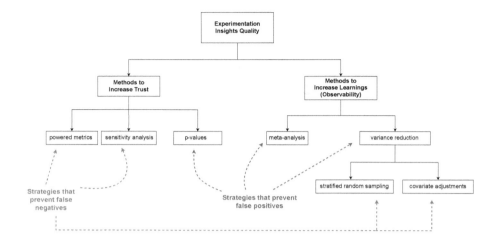

otherwise go unnoticed. Ensuring your test has adequate statistical power is critical to identifying real changes and avoiding missed opportunities. And just like with false positives, variance reduction techniques play a dual role, reducing variability in the data to help uncover true positives.

By including these strategies in your experimentation practices, you're creating a strong foundation to minimize errors in your A/B tests. This not only leads to more trustworthy results but also ensures that every experiment contributes meaningful, actionable insights to guide your product decisions.

Chapter Roundup: Verifying You're Measuring True Effect

It's easy to jump to conclusions and celebrate promising experiment results. But before you do, it's best to double-check that insights gathered from the experiment are not false positives. It's better to double down now than to realize months later that you've influenced the user experience or product roadmap with misinformed insights.

Use the following checklist to verify you've generated quality and trustworthy insights that you can then use to influence product and engineering decisions.

1. Verify the statistical power of the experiment to ensure metrics were not underpowered.

2. Implement variance reduction strategies, such as covariate adjustments and stratified random sampling, to increase sensitivity and gain even more insights from each experiment.

3. Consider replicating the experiment with a higher p-value to reduce the false positive risk.

4. Compare results to similar experiments by conducting meta-analysis. If this experiment metrics gains are suspiciously higher, consider running for a longer duration to combat false positive risk.

Like any tool, it's important to use the tool correctly. A/B testing is a tool that can help your product and engineering organization evaluate options so you can make better and more informed decisions. Make sure you are using this tool correctly by doubling down on experimentation quality.

Wrapping Up

The more insights you can gather from an experiment, the more informed you'll be as you decide whether to launch the feature to all your users. A/B testing is costly because it takes time and engineering resources to enable. The more product and user insights you gain from an experiment, the more likely your engineering organization will prioritize investments in your experimentation platform.

In this chapter, you explored how to increase insight quality so you can learn more from the experiments executed on your A/B testing platform. The tactics that can increase insights include the following:

• Replicate experiments to combat the experiments that may have suggested a false positive result.

• Introduce variance reduction strategies to increase sensitivity of test results.

• Increase trust in your experiments by avoiding mistakes like underpowering metrics and by extending experiment durations to decrease false positive risk.

Now that you're familiar with strategies to improve experimentation quality, let's tackle another thorny issue in A/B testing: holdbacks. In the next chapter, we'll discuss the problems with long-term holdbacks and practice some less expensive alternative approaches.

CHAPTER 7

Practicing Adaptive Testing Strategies

In this chapter, we'll build on concepts you're already familiar with. For instance, multi-armed bandit testing dynamically shifts more traffic to the better-performing variant while continuing to explore other options. Sequential testing takes a different approach, monitoring results in real time and using statistical thresholds to decide whether to stop or continue. Both fall under the broader category of adaptive testing strategies.

This chapter expands on what you've learned so far, diving deeper into the context and practical applications of adaptive testing.

Here's what we'll cover:

- Fundamentals of sequential testing and how it relates to adaptive testing.

- Data infrastructure needed to support adaptive testing strategies.

- High-level logical flow and components of implementing a multi-armed bandit.

- Tooling changes to incorporate adaptive testing strategies into your experimentation workflow.

Adaptive testing is an incredibly powerful tool, making it well worth dedicating an entire chapter to explore—but first, let's pause to discuss an important caveat.

Navigating the Potential of Adaptive Testing Strategies

Before we dive into the details, it's good to set expectations. Adaptive testing methods, like multi-armed bandits and Thompson sampling, are compelling strategies that can elevate your experimentation practices to new heights. These methods allow you to dynamically adjust traffic and optimize in real time, unlocking opportunities for improved outcomes. However, adaptive testing often demands significant engineering, research, and data infrastructure. While some of the most advanced companies have embraced adaptive testing as part of their playbook, others equally advanced have opted not to incorporate it, as it doesn't make sense for their product.

That doesn't mean you shouldn't explore adaptive testing. On the contrary, understanding these advanced techniques is important, as it could influence your overall experimentation strategy down the road. Even if you decide not to incorporate adaptive testing into your experimentation practices right away, knowing when and how it can make a difference sets you up to identify the right opportunities in the future.

Taking your experimentation practices to the next level isn't about using every method out there—it's about finding the strategies that work for your team, your product, and your experimentation goal. As we move forward, keep an open mind and consider how these strategies could align with your needs.

With that said, let's jump in and break down what adaptive testing entails.

What Is Adaptive Testing?

Let's say you're hosting a party. You're unsure what snacks your guests prefer, so you prepare stuffed mushrooms and mini–potato skins. You monitor your guests' reactions to each snack as the night evolves. You start noticing that more guests are enjoying the stuffed mushrooms, so you start putting more stuffed mushrooms in the oven while heating up fewer mini-potato skins.

Adjusting the snacks available at your party based on observing your guest's actions in real time is an analogy for adaptive testing. You continuously learned from your guests what they preferred and then adjusted what was cooked throughout the night, not after the fact.

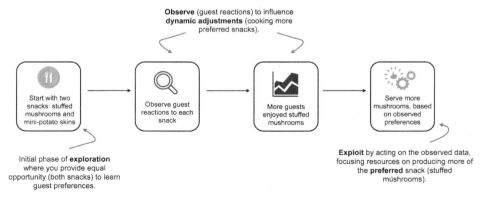

For an experiment on a product, adaptive A/B testing strategies aim to expose more users to the better-performing variant, similar to ensuring that guests end up eating the dish they prefer the most. If you were running a classic split A/B test, you would serve both snacks throughout the party and only evaluate their performance afterward by seeing which snack guests ate more of, using that information to plan future parties.

Adaptive A/B testing allows the allocation of users and traffic within an online controlled experiment to be dynamically adjusted based on real-time data. How this compares to classic A/B testing is simple: the traffic split between variants remains fixed from start to finish. See the following image that visualizes classic A/B testing to adaptive testing with a specific focus on user exposure allocation differences between the two strategies.

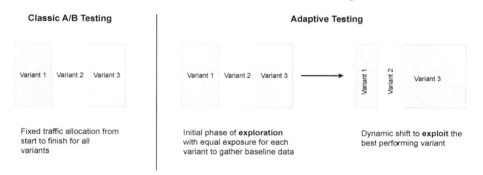

It's important to highlight a key best practice: avoid touching or editing the configuration of a traditional A/B test once it has started. Changes, such as altering user targeting criteria after users have already been exposed, can disrupt critical factors like logging and metrics calculation, potentially leading to issues such as the unintended exclusion of users and compromised results. Even for adaptive testing strategies, the experimentation platform should facilitate the dynamic adjustment of traffic based on real-time engagement data (in comparison to a human editing the test allocation details).

With a basic understanding of adaptive testing in mind, let's get into the benefits of adopting such a strategy.

Benefitting from Adaptive Testing

The primary benefit of adaptive testing is its ability to dynamically allocate traffic based on observed performance, enabling greater exposure to the best-performing variant. Take note of the words "observed performance" in the previous sentence—this distinction is crucial. Adaptive testing relies on the data it collects in real time, which means decisions are made based on noisy, potentially incomplete signals. Unlike traditional A/B testing, which prioritizes statistical confidence before acting, adaptive methods are optimized for learning and reacting quickly. This tradeoff—between fast adaptation and statistical rigor—underscores why adaptive testing excels in some scenarios but may fall short in others, especially when unbiased estimation is critical.

The two primary reasons for implementing adaptive testing to evaluate changes in a product are these:

1. When time or traffic is limited, making it important to learn and act quickly.

2. When there's a need to maximize reward, particularly in high-opportunity-cost environments where running a suboptimal variant for too long could lead to significant losses.

Additionally, adaptive algorithms—such as contextual bandits—can learn from user behavior in real time, enabling personalized decision-making and driving longer-term optimization.

Varying Types of Adaptive Testing

In most cases, when someone refers to adaptive testing, they're typically thinking of dynamic traffic allocation strategies. However, the term can be defined more broadly—as any method that modifies the traditional A/B testing process. Under this broader definition, sequential A/B testing can also be considered a form of adaptive testing. Sequential testing involves monitoring performance and potentially stopping a test early based on interim results.

In Chapter 2, Improving Experimentation Throughput, on page 25, we discussed sequential testing in relation to different types of experiments and how each type influences the testing capacity within the product. In this chapter, we'll dig in a bit deeper into all the details needed to support sequential testing and how it falls within the adaptive testing umbrella.

These are the distinct strategies we'll explore in this chapter:

*   Sequential testing
*   Multi-armed bandits
*   Thompson sampling
*   Contextual bandits

All these methods involve making decisions as you gather new data during the evaluation and offer a different balance between speed, precision, and complexity. Each method differs in how it incorporates and models uncertainty. Which adaptive testing strategy you select depends on the problem you're solving, the amount of traffic, and the trade-offs you're willing to make between exploration and exploitation.

A key differentiator among these strategies lies in how they model uncertainty. For example, multi-armed bandits use reward-based feedback to dynamically allocate traffic, aiming to exploit what works best while still exploring less certain options.

Thompson sampling is an algorithm for solving the multi-armed bandit problem. It uses probabilistic modeling to manage uncertainty and strikes a balance between exploring new options and exploiting what's already working. The algorithm adjusts dynamically based on how likely each variant is to be the best choice.

Contextual bandits take this a step further by introducing user-specific data into the decision-making framework. By leveraging datasets that include user features, it enables more personalized decisions, tailoring the experience to individual users rather than treating everyone the same.

Let's explore where these common adaptive testing strategies fit in, starting with sequential testing, as it's less similar to the algorithmic and model-heavy adaptive testing approaches.

Making Decisions Early with Sequential Testing

Sequential experiments are a form of hypothesis testing that can conclude early (compared to a classic fixed-horizon A/B test). With this approach, your A/B test still has a fixed end date, but you gain the option to stop early.

Let's revisit the sequential testing strategy at a high level. This method consists of the following:

- Monitoring and analyzing data while the experiment is active.
- Stopping or continuing the experiment depending on the data captured, possibly ending early if the results are statistically significant or if there's clear evidence that one variant is superior.

While the multi-armed bandit and Thompson sampling algorithms focus on dynamically allocating traffic based on a reward, sequential testing focuses on continuously observing data with the potential opportunity to stop the experiment early if there's enough evidence. The decision to stop or continue is adaptive, depending on how the data looks at each checkpoint. If a large effect is observed early on, the test can be stopped, conserving resources that can unlock other experiments.

Another reason sequential testing can be considered adaptive is its flexible sample size. Unlike traditional fixed-sample testing, where the sample size and stopping criteria are predefined before the experiment starts, sequential testing involves continuously monitoring the data in real time. Based on the interim data observed during the active experiment, you can make decisions to potentially continue running or stop the experiment early.

In general, the experiment's flexibility, efficiency, and continuous monitoring make the sequential testing strategy adaptive.

Enabling Sequential Testing

In practice, the sequential testing strategy requires a combination of statistics, planning, and engineering infrastructure to be incorporated into your experimentation practices. As you'll see throughout this chapter, this trifecta is required for all testing strategies. Let's expand on this with a broad guide for performing sequential testing.

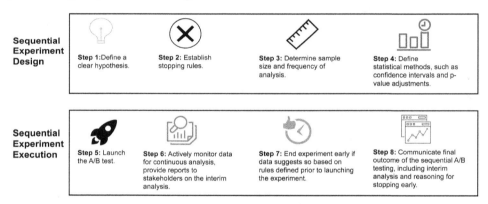

As you can see from the previous image, two concepts are absent that are key to the classic fixed-horizon A/B tests: establishing stopping rules and frequency of analysis.

You might decide to stop a sequential test early for two main reasons:

1. When there's enough data to clearly show that one variant is performing better.

2. When it becomes evident that it's unlikely to detect a meaningful difference between the variants.

To make this strategy for online experimentation reliable, you'll need to establish statistical boundaries as part of your early stopping rules. These boundaries help control false positives and ensure your insights are accurate.

Here's how it works in practice: first, you define the stopping boundaries for both scenarios—when to stop because one variant is superior and when to stop due to a lack of meaningful differences. Next, as the experiment runs, you analyze the data at predefined checkpoints and compare it to the boundaries. Finally, based on what the data tells you at each checkpoint, you decide whether to continue the test or stop it early. It's all about balancing the need for reliable results with efficient use of time and resources. If you're wondering how these statistical boundaries are set, this is where your trusty data scientist can help. They might mention techniques like O'Brien-Fleming or Pocock boundaries, which are commonly used to establish these thresholds.

As for how often you conduct interim analysis, you have two options. You can predefine checkpoints based on time or number of users allocated to the experiment—for instance, performing interim analysis every N days. Or you can conduct interim analysis based on specific events. Having dashboards so you can quickly and frequently peek at your experiment is critical to making this approach sustainable and scalable.

Speaking of dashboards, it's worth considering masking specific experiment details in your results to prevent bias. Let's explore that concept further in the next section.

Masking Interim Analysis to Prevent Bias

We're all susceptible to bias in one way or another. Sometimes, teams build features purely based on product strategy (that's hopefully anchored on user research), regardless of whether they believe in the effectiveness of the feature. Other times, teams are deeply invested in features they believe must be launched—perhaps because so much effort went into the model design that shelving it would feel like a loss. This kind of conviction can increase the risk of biased interpretation, especially when looking at data early in a sequential experiment. Teams may subconsciously interpret results in a way that supports their desired outcome.

One way to mitigate this is through tooling: if teams can peek at data during a running experiment, consider masking the test cell or variant names in the results. This simple practice can help reduce bias during active monitoring. See the image shown on page 144.

Like all experimentation strategies, putting the time and energy up front toward designing the experiment itself always pays off. The more details you think through early on, the better prepared you'll be to interpret the results and make decisions.

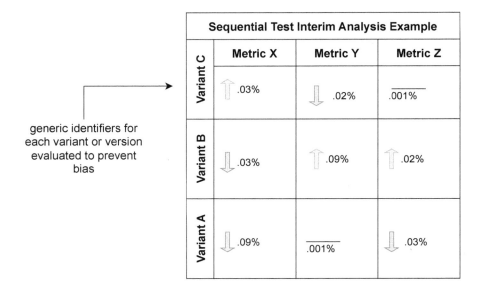

generic identifiers for each variant or version evaluated to prevent bias

Sequential Test Interim Analysis Example			
	Metric X	Metric Y	Metric Z
Variant C	⬆ .03%	⬇ .02%	‾‾ .001%
Variant B	⬇ .03%	⬆ .09%	⬆ .02%
Variant A	⬇ .09%	‾‾ .001%	⬇ .03%

Making Multi-Armed Bandits Effective for You

As you already know from Chapter 4, Improving Machine Learning Evaluation Practices, on page 75, multi-armed bandits (MAB) aim to balance exploration by trying different variants while exploiting to maximize reward. To quickly refresh your memory, here's what a multi-armed bandit at a high level consists of:

1. *Exploration.* Users are introduced to different "arms," actions or variants to understand their impact and effect.

2. *Exploitation.* Based on the data from exploration, the next step is to select the variant currently estimated to have the highest expected reward to maximize immediate gains.

3. *Balancing the exploration and exploitation.* This critical step finds the right balance. For example, if you explore too much, you'll miss out on exploiting the variant that will result in the highest reward. Or if you exploit too much, you may miss out on discovering another variant with a higher reward.

For the last step, strategies such as Thompson sampling are used to strike this balancing act effectively. We'll explore Thompson sampling in an upcoming section. Until then, let's take this theory and see what's needed to support a multi-armed bandit in practice.

Engineer Task: Conceptualizing a Multi-Armed Bandit

Exploration, exploitation, and balancing the two are steps that work iteratively to maximize reward over time, continuously learning from the outcomes of the winning arms. While this sounds great in theory, how would you actually conceptualize the multi-armed bandit framework? Or said otherwise, how would you define the high-level steps if you were to break down the work needed to design a multi-armed bandit? The goal of this exercise is not to build a multi-armed bandit but rather to gain a deep understanding of the high-level approach so you're well prepared to pitch this strategy as part of your experimentation roadmap.

> **Engineer Task:** What are the high-level steps to design a multi-armed bandit?

Since we're working with a strategy that's more complex than the classic A/B test you're already familiar with, let's break the multi-armed bandit approach into two phases: design and implementation. In the design phase, you'll focus on defining the objective and identifying the arms and rewards—both of which play a key role in selecting the right bandit algorithm. In the implementation phase, you'll move into building the algorithm, integrating it into your production experimentation workflow, setting up dynamic traffic allocation, and figuring out the timing and methods for analyzing the data.

The following diagram illustrates the key steps within the two phases, where the goal is to define at a high level the logic needed to design a multi-armed bandit framework.

Multi-Armed Bandit Design	**Step 1:** Define a clear objective and metrics.	**Step 2:** Implement a bandit algorithm such as epsilon-greedy, Thompson sampling, or contextual bandits if you have user features.	**Step 3:** Determine the number of arms or variants to experiment with.	**Step 4:** Define constraints on exploration, like budget limits or maximum exposure for each variation.
Multi-Armed Bandit Execution	**Step 5:** Integrate the bandit algorithm with the engineering system that enables the feature on the product.	**Step 6:** Implement the logic to dynamically allocate traffic to different variations based on the bandit algorithm's recommendations.	**Step 7:** Periodically evaluate and adjust the parameters of the bandit algorithm, such as exploration rates, if necessary. Continuously analyze data to understand the performance of each variation.	**Step 8:** Depending on your use case, you may have the algorithm continuously learning or you may settle on a winner.

Similar to the first step in almost every experimentation strategy, you need a clear objective—define what you aim to optimize, such as click-through rate, revenue, or conversions. Defining the correct measurement for success is important for every test, especially a multi-armed bandit where the objective influences what is exploited.

Significant differences exist between multi-armed bandits and A/B tests. Both are used for experimentation, and both have a number of changes evaluated at once—where an "arm" in a multi-armed bandit is similar to a variant in an A/B test. The difference is in the implementation. In a multi-armed bandit the algorithm chooses between each arm to maximize learning efficiency by either exploiting known good arms or exploring new ones to gather more information. Whereas an A/B test splits traffic evenly, and you wait to make a decision after the experiment concludes, multi-armed bandits are more dynamic and adaptive, as you are continuously optimizing performance during the experiment.

As a reminder, illustrating advanced topics in a practical way is the focus of this book. While implementing a multi-armed bandit involves additional complexities—such as selecting the appropriate algorithm (Thompson sampling or epsilon-greedy), defining prior distributions, tuning exploration-exploitation trade-offs, and handling edge cases like cold starts—those finer algorithmic and mathematical details are better suited for another book focused specifically on the algorithmic aspects of experimentation. In the meantime, let's get back to the practical aspects of a multi-armed bandit. For example, you might be wondering, since classic A/B tests have a clear end date, does a multi-armed bandit evaluation ever conclude? It depends. Let's explore multi-armed bandits further in the next section.

Learning Continuously Versus Launching a Winner Variant

Whether your multi-armed bandit is always running or eventually settling on a winner depends on your goals and implementation.

In some situations, a multi-armed bandit algorithm is continuously learning, adjusting traffic to different variants over time. The algorithm is never settling on a winner; it's enabling a dynamic environment where data or user preferences may evolve and a continuous optimization to maximize reward is desired.

An example of where this would be applied is e-commerce platforms. To stay competitive and meet customer demand, you can test different price points for the same product to find the optimal price as the multi-armed bandit continuously learns and adapts the pricing in real time. Online advertising is another ideal application of a continuously learning multi-armed bandit approach; the effectiveness of ads can vary based on time, user, and news events, so having a multi-armed bandit in place, maximizing return on those ads, will increase relevance and effectiveness.

Other scenarios are where the focus is on finding the best variant and deploying that version to all users, such as launching a new product or creating a new feature where multiple designs are evaluated. Your multi-armed bandit algorithm is used to determine the most effective design. The algorithm tests the various designs over a fixed period and then selects the best-performing design for a full rollout to all users.

Selecting a winner is also ideal when there's a fixed time period, such as seasonal promotions. For example, retailers often test various promotions during the holiday season on their websites, including a fixed test period to determine the most effective promotion, which is then used for the remainder of the season.

In these examples, the multi-armed bandit is configured to converge on a single best-performing variant after a certain period or once enough data is captured to make a decision. Once the algorithm identifies the winning variant, the exploration phase ends, and the winner is deployed to all users.

Prioritizing Production Requirements

Let's say you're an avid baker. You'll have situations where something went wrong on a long-enough timeline. Whether you fail to measure an ingredient correctly or the oven isn't working as expected, there's always a chance for errors.

Similarly, deploying a multi-armed bandit into a production setting does come with its own challenges—mainly impacting the effectiveness of this experimentation strategy.

The first and most common error is insufficient exploration when the algorithm settles too quickly on a suboptimal option. This can happen when the algorithm focuses too heavily on exploitation and not enough on trying new variants (exploration); it could miss out on identifying the ideal variant leading to suboptimal long-term performance.

While the effectiveness of your algorithm is important, enabling it to scale is equally relevant in a production setting. Multi-armed bandit algorithms require significant computational resources, especially compared to a classic A/B test experiment. If the algorithm needs to process a large amount of data, you'll need to scale your infrastructure to support that requirement, which will naturally also impact your operational cost. Similarly, a complex algorithm might lead to slower performance, making it useless for real-time applications.

When choosing a bandit algorithm, it's important to consider how quickly the algorithm can adapt, as this directly affects how well it balances exploration (trying different options) and exploitation (favoring the best-performing option). A faster-adapting algorithm can reduce regret—the difference between the actual reward obtained and the reward that would have been earned by always selecting the best variant—by more quickly shifting traffic to the ideal choice as user behavior or conditions change. Ironically (or perhaps not so ironically), one of the more adaptive strategies is Thompson sampling—which we'll explore next!

Opting for Thompson Sampling Algorithm

Now that you're familiar with the adaptive testing strategy of multi-armed bandits, let's dive into one of the most popular algorithms used in this approach: Thompson sampling. Unlike predefined logic or deterministic rules, the Thompson sampling algorithm makes decisions based on probability distributions of possible outcomes.

Returning to a food analogy, imagine you're at a buffet with several dishes you haven't tried yet. As a curious foodie, you want to find the most delicious dish. Instead of sampling dishes randomly or sticking with one that looks promising, you use a probabilistic approach. For each dish, you estimate the likelihood of it being your favorite based on factors like previous tastings, reviews, or even your instincts.

With these estimates, you choose your next dish by sampling from the probability distributions. This method balances exploration (trying new dishes you haven't tasted yet) with exploitation (revisiting dishes you already know you like). The key is that your decision-making process is guided by probabilities, allowing you to refine your choices as you gather more data.

In the context of experimentation, this approach mirrors how Thompson sampling allocates traffic to test variants in a multi-armed bandit. Instead of testing each variant equally or relying on predefined logic, the algorithm dynamically adjusts based on which variant is most likely to perform better while still giving other variants a chance to prove themselves.

If your experimentation platform has limited computational resources or needs to scale across a large user base, Thompson sampling is a particularly good choice. Its efficiency and adaptability make it well suited for large-scale, resource-constrained environments where running intensive algorithms isn't feasible.

At a very high level, to implement Thompson sampling, you need the following practical components, illustrated in the following image.

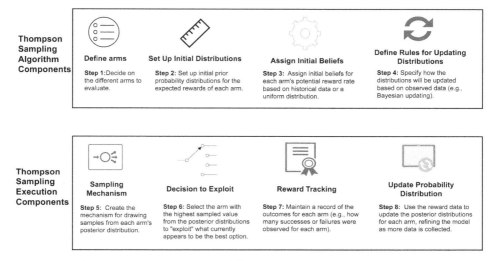

This image breaks down the logical flow and components of implementing a Thompson sampling algorithm. It starts with the foundational pieces, like defining arms, setting up priors, and establishing rules for updating distributions. Then it moves into the execution phase, covering key actions such as sampling, exploiting the best options, and refining distributions based on outcomes. Together, these steps provide a clear picture of how Thompson sampling works in practice.

Engineer Task: Applying Thompson Sampling at MarketMax

Thompson sampling is an effective algorithm for addressing the exploration-exploitation trade-off in multi-armed bandits. This trade-off is about balancing the need to explore new options (to learn which one performs best) with exploiting the best-performing option (to maximize rewards). For example, suppose you're running an A/B test on a website with multiple designs and aren't sure which will perform better. Using probabilistic modeling—which applies probability distributions to predict and manage uncertainty—you can test both designs. Over time, Thompson sampling gradually favors the design that's performing better, while still allocating some traffic to the other design to ensure its performance isn't being underestimated.

Now, how does this apply to MarketMax? MarketMax customers shop for craft goods on its website, and product teams frequently experiment with features to improve user experience and boost sales. Thompson sampling could be particularly useful in scenarios where MarketMax wants to optimize features dynamically, such as testing different product recommendations, home page layouts, or even pricing strategies. By gradually favoring the better-performing options while still exploring others, MarketMax could maximize its success while continuously learning about customer preferences. Let's brainstorm practical applications for the Thompson sampling algorithm at MarketMax.

 Engineer Task: What are practical applications at MarketMax for implementing a multi-armed bandit using the Thompson sampling algorithm?

The most practical use case for the Thompson sampling algorithm within a multi-armed bandit is to optimize product recommendations to maximize sales or customer engagement. Let's illustrate how this could be structured by starting with the objective.

The first step is to define an objective. In the context of MarketMax, the objective could be to maximize craft goods purchases by recommending the most appealing products to customers visiting the website.

The second step would be to define the arms, where each arm of the bandit algorithm represents a different product or category of products, such as in the following example:

- *Arm 1.* Handmade jewelry recommendations.
- *Arm 2.* Home decor recommendations.
- *Arm 3.* Art supplies recommendations.
- *Arm 4.* Seasonal product recommendations.

The third step would be to implement the Thompson sampling algorithm to determine which arm would be selected to direct traffic to. The next step includes enabling data collection to be fed to the algorithm to measure the objective (purchases for each arm) and updating the success rate based on the data collected. Since the Thompson sampling algorithm balances exploration and exploitation, over time, as you collect more data, the recommendations served on the MarketMax website will become increasingly tailored and effective, allowing you to utilize the adaptive and self-optimizing nature of Thompson sampling to make real-time decisions to evaluate the different recommendations options.

Now, you may be wondering if there's a way to further personalize which arm a user selects in a multi-armed bandit. Luckily, that's exactly what we'll explore next with contextual bandits.

Personalizing the Decision with Contextual Bandits

Contextual bandits are a type of multi-armed bandit but with an added layer of complexity that involves using relevant data, such as user attributes, to make decisions. In a standard multi-armed bandit design, you choose between different arms based on their performance, without considering any external information about the user or environment. Said otherwise, in a standard multi-armed bandit solution, every user is treated the same, and data or information related to the user is not leveraged to determine which arm to direct traffic to.

However, in contextual bandits, the algorithm considers contextual data before determining which arm to select (allocate traffic to). For example, contextual data can be defined as user attributes, timestamps, and device types (browser vs. mobile). The goal is to personalize the decision-making process based on the current contextual data to optimize the outcome.

Let's illustrate the difference with an example at MarketMax. If you were to implement a multi-armed bandit to evaluate various versions of a marketing email to promote products on the MarketMax website, you would direct traffic to each version purely based on historical click-through rate. Now let's say you have access to user-specific data, such as past interactions or location. Then you would use that data to help decide which email version to send so you can personalize the outcome and hopefully improve performance.

By leveraging user-oriented data, contextual bandits can improve the accuracy and relevance of decisions in situations where users respond differently to various arms, such as personalized recommendations, marketing campaigns, and dynamic pricing on e-commerce sites.

Generalizing Components to Support Adaptive Testing

Now is the perfect time to examine the commonality in infrastructure, tooling, and implementation of each adaptive testing strategy. The choice of which adaptive testing strategy depends on several factors, including the problem you're solving, the amount of traffic available, and the nature of the trade-offs you're willing to make. If you have limited traffic and a need for precision, sequential testing or Thompson sampling might be preferable. If speed is your top priority and you can tolerate a higher level of uncertainty, a multi-armed bandit approach might suffice. When personalization is desired, contextual bandits are often the best choice.

No matter which adaptive testing framework you implement, you'll need real-time data, more dashboards, visualizations to understand what's happening in production, and tooling to configure your evaluations. Once you take the leap to implement adaptive testing strategies on your product, you can leverage these shared components as you pick and choose which methods work best for your use case. See the following table for a generalization of how each strategy compares.

	Sequential Testing	Multi-Armed Bandit	Thompson Sampling Algorithm	Contextual Bandit
Exploration vs. Exploitation	No	Yes	Yes	Yes
Are decisions made as the data comes in?	Yes	Yes	Yes	Yes
Is this a probabilistic approach?	No	Yes	Yes	Yes
Is there a model or heuristic making predictions and guiding decisions?	No	Yes	Yes	Yes
Are user attributes used to help decide which variant to direct traffic to?	No	No	No, unless it's a contextual Thompson sampling algorithm	Yes
Is this a type of multi-armed bandit?	No, more aligned with hypothesis testing and controlled experimentation	--	Yes	Yes, extends the basic MAB problem by adding context

Let's summarize some of the key points illustrated in the strategy comparison table. Sequential testing doesn't involve the balance between exploration and exploitation like multi-armed bandits, Thompson sampling, and contextual bandits do—that's a big difference in how these methods work. All of them, though, are dynamic and allow decisions to be made as data comes in, which is what makes them so powerful. Unlike the others, sequential testing isn't probabilistic or based on predictive models—it's more straightforward in that sense. Sequential testing stands out from other adaptive testing strategies because it closely resembles a classic A/B test, relying on the traditional statistical hypothesis testing framework. What really sets contextual bandits apart is how they use user attributes to guide decisions, adding a layer of personalization that the other methods don't have. Each methodology requires real-time data to make decisions, which is the perfect segue into the following section.

Anchoring on Data Infrastructure

Beyond the statistical and algorithmic aspects required for adaptive testing, supporting multi-armed bandits and sequential testing requires a fair amount of engineering infrastructure. Luckily, a good amount of the infrastructure should be available through your experimentation platform, but it's worth emphasizing the data infrastructure unique to implementing adaptive testing.

First, you'll need a system that collects and stores data, such as interactions or outcomes, from each arm of a multi-armed bandit. This data provides a feedback loop to update the algorithm's estimated reward based on the observed outcomes. For instance, if an arm performs well, its estimated reward may increase, influencing its chances of exploitation.

This continuous feedback loop is iterative, requiring data collection and algorithm updates throughout the evaluation so your multi-armed bandit can adapt to reach peak reward.

Think about the weight and importance of this data infrastructure. Traditionally, user engagement data is used for monitoring and test analysis, but now it's also a core component that enables the experimentation methodology itself. In some cases, an experimentation platform that just supports classic fixed-horizon A/B tests may collect and compute metrics daily, but for a multi-armed bandit, you'd ideally want to increase the frequency. Real-time data processing is crucial for adaptive testing to enable timely decision-making, such as reallocating traffic or stopping experiments early. This contrasts with fixed-horizon A/B tests, where metrics can often be computed in batch processes.

A well-architected, scalable data platform is the backbone of adaptive testing, ensuring real-time processing, reliable feedback loops, and the capacity to handle growing demands seamlessly.

Extending Tooling for Adaptive Testing Needs

It's much easier to build a tool that can enable a classic A/B test; it's a bit harder to incorporate more advanced strategies, such as adaptive testing implementations. The better your experimentation tooling is, the less teams have to think or do up front to run a well-designed experiment. No matter what type of organization you're in, it's challenging to scale the experimentation domain knowledge to all teams, so tooling plays a significant role in enabling different experimentation strategies on a product.

The user interfaces that support the experimentation methodologies available for teams to use when they have features to evaluate should include additional views to support adaptive testing. For the sequential testing use case, dashboards or visualizations enabling you to interpret interim insights during an active experiment are required.

Depending on how self-service you want to make your multi-armed bandit approach, it influences the capabilities you add to your experimentation platform user interface. You can start simply by having the arms, rewards, and other factors critical to a multi-armed bandit be defined via configuration files or a dynamic property management tool. However, if you plan on platformizing multi-armed bandits, incorporating ways to configure and monitor the evaluation would reduce the burden on engineers supporting updates or answering status questions.

For instance, consider adding the following capabilities to your experimentation platform user interface to platformize multi-armed bandits:

- *Experiment setup.* Teams should be able to define different arms or variants, the objective and how reward is measured, and tuning parameters that influence exploitation and exploration balancing.

- *Real-time monitoring.* Teams should be able to view metrics for each arm that align with the reward definition.

- *Algorithm status.* Teams should be able to see the progress in the various phases of a multi-armed bandit, such as which arm is currently being exploited or what the exploration rate is.

Tooling, data and operational constraints of your experimentation platform, and your tolerance for the risks associated with exploration and exploitation are all factors you should keep top of mind as you incorporate adaptive testing into your experimentation practices. Incorporating adaptive testing requires a thoughtful approach that balances the complexity with the accessibility for teams that run experiments on the product. The ultimate goal is to implement these strategies that not only support advanced methodologies but also make them approachable, enabling teams to leverage these powerful tools to drive innovation and informed decision-making at scale.

Chapter Roundup: Engineering Team Requirements to Support Adaptive Testing

For a quick moment, let's return to why adaptive testing can take your experimentation practices to the next level. Unlike classic A/B tests, adaptive testing can maximize the metrics gains by dynamically adjusting traffic allocation across multiple variants. However, there's a clear tradeoff here—you're increasing the potential for reward while adding complexity to your engineering system. For example, consider the on-call engineer who must quickly address issues with the real-time data processing pipeline to ensure the multi-armed bandit algorithm isn't working with stale data. These challenges aren't meant to deter you from implementing adaptive testing strategies but rather to highlight the importance of having well-defined use cases to justify the added complexity.

Whether you're an engineering leader looking to elevate your experimentation practices, a lead engineer eager to drive innovation one experimentation strategy at a time, or a product owner shaping your roadmap and considering adaptive testing, the key is ensuring your team has the right domain expertise. Regardless of what your role is, you need to make sure you have the right domain skill sets to take your experimentation practices to the next level.

Use the following list as a reference for what needs to be in place, from an engineering organization's point of view, to support this more complex experimentation strategy.

- Data engineers to support the data infrastructure necessary for collecting, storing, and processing data to inform adaptive testing decisions and algorithms.

- Data scientists to implement the statistical rigor, algorithms, and visualizations illustrating insights from the evaluations.

- UX designers to help create user-friendly tooling.

- Engineers to incorporate the core logic into your experimentation or production architecture.

- Product management to create requirements and platformize the testing strategies so teams across a company can benefit from them.

With these skill sets, you'll be able to build out the adaptive testing strategies of your dreams.

Wrapping Up

You've made it to the end of a jam-packed chapter—nicely done! By introducing several methodologies, such as sequential testing, multi-armed bandits, Thompson sampling, and contextual bandits, you're armed with the knowledge to advance experimentation practices beyond the classic A/B tests.

Here's a quick recap of the key takeaways from this chapter:

- Dynamically adjusting the testing process in real time by implementing adaptive testing strategies contrasts sharply with traditional fixed-horizon A/B tests.

- Maximizing rewards, optimizing resource use, and improving decision-making speed highlight the benefits of adaptive testing.

- Building robust engineering and data infrastructure enables real-time processing, dashboards, and algorithmic decision-making.

- Implementing sequential testing gives you the flexibility to stop early if the data provides clear answers along the way while still having a defined end date.

- Balancing exploration and exploitation defines the core strategies of sequential testing, multi-armed bandits, Thompson sampling, and contextual bandits.

- Assembling a multidisciplinary team ensures the successful implementation and scalability of adaptive testing strategies.

Now that you have a lens into adaptive testing strategies, we can tackle a popular yet somewhat thorny experimentation problem space: long-term evaluations, such as holdbacks. In the next chapter, we'll talk about the benefits and pitfalls of long-term holdbacks and explore some less expensive alternative approaches.

CHAPTER 8

Measuring Long-Term Impact

Up until this point, you've got a good grasp of strategies you can implement to up-level how you compare the performance of two or more variants over a relatively short period. For example, in the previous chapter we discussed adaptive testing strategies that can enable you to allocate traffic dynamically to exploit the best-performing variant for immediate gains. In contrast, long-term evaluation strategies, such as long-term holdbacks, focus on measuring sustained or delayed effects, like user retention, over a more extended period. Now, it's time to explore long-term evaluations and how they can measure sustained or delayed effects.

Measuring long-term effect is a classic topic in the experimentation realm with very practical limitations. We'll explore the pitfalls and benefits of classic long-term evaluation strategies, such as holdbacks and post-period analysis.

More specifically, this chapter explores the following:

- Implementing and maintaining long-term holdbacks to measure sustained impact while addressing their challenges.

- Conducting post-period analysis to evaluate feature performance after rollout, balancing simplicity and accuracy.

- Using continuous monitoring to track feature performance over time and identify unexpected trends or issues.

- Leveraging predictive CLV models to gain early insights into long-term impact and complement other strategies.

- Balancing cost, complexity, and practicality to select the right long-term evaluation approach for your organization.

It's important to measure the long-term impact of features and iterations on a user-facing product. Some metrics, such as customer lifetime value, retention, and churn, take time to reflect the true impact of a change; immediate effects seen in short-term A/B tests might not represent the eventual long-term impact. Let's get into the complex but crucial topic of long-term evaluations.

Why You Should Measure Long-Term Impact

Imagine you're perfecting your slow-cooked stew recipe, tweaking the spices and ingredient proportions. From experience, you know that the richness, texture, and flavors result from several hours of cooking. However, if you wanted to get an idea of how good the stew is, you could taste it early on, such as 10 minutes into the cooking time. The taste at this early checkpoint gives you an initial insight into what's happening, but it's far from the final result. For example, you know after 10 minutes that you didn't add too much salt, which is good! But you're unsure of the texture, so you need more time to gauge it.

If we translate this food analogy to the experimentation domain, the short-term checkpoint of whether the stew has too much salt, for example, gives you a rough idea, but it doesn't give you the complete picture of the flavor profile of the changes you made to the stew recipe. Once you let the stew cook thoroughly for hours, you'll get a true reflection of the changes you've made.

The following timeline illustrates a direct parallel between the stages of cooking the stew and the stages of experimentation, emphasizing the differences between short-term and long-term evaluations.

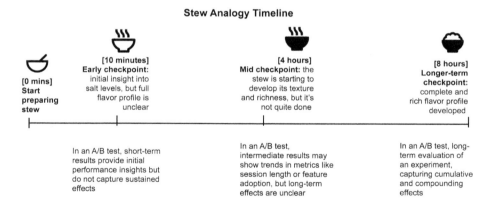

Stew Analogy Timeline

| | [10 minutes] Early checkpoint: initial insight into salt levels, but full flavor profile is unclear | [4 hours] Mid checkpoint: the stew is starting to develop its texture and richness, but it's not quite done | [8 hours] Longer-term checkpoint: complete and rich flavor profile developed |

[0 mins] Start preparing stew

In an A/B test, short-term results provide initial performance insights but do not capture sustained effects

In an A/B test, intermediate results may show trends in metrics like session length or feature adoption, but long-term effects are unclear

In an A/B test, long-term evaluation of an experiment, capturing cumulative and compounding effects

When iterating on a product, a change that may provide short-term improvements in user engagement can have hidden long-term consequences, such as user fatigue, dissatisfaction, or increased churn. If you're measuring only the immediate impact, it's like judging the taste of the dish by the first few bites as the dish continues to stew. To truly understand the effect of a product change or new feature, you must measure how it plays out over a longer timeline—whether it continues delivering value or leads to unintended negative outcomes.

In previous chapters, we focused on experimentation strategies designed to measure effects over shorter timelines or to evaluate feature-level metrics. To transition into the topic of long-term evaluations, the following table provides a high-level comparison of long-term evaluations versus short-term A/B tests. This high-level overview illustrates key differences, offering a foundational understanding before we dive deeper into the details of long-term evaluation strategies.

	Long-Term Evaluations	Shorter-Term A/B Test
Duration	• Typically months to observe delayed or compounding effects.	• Typically runs for a few days or weeks, depending on traffic, goals, and product.
Primary Use Case	• Evaluations that capture delayed and compounding effects.	• Evaluating product changes against feature level metrics.
Challenges	• Higher engineering cost. • Risk for production incidents due to complexity. • Increased resource demands.	• Risk of novelty effects and seasonal biases. • Misleading results due to temporary effects.
Example Metrics	• Top-line company metrics, such as retention, customer lifetime value, or revenue over time.	• Feature-level metrics such as click-through or conversion rates.

The main reasons product and engineering teams often skip measuring long-term impact are cost and practicality. First, maintaining a long-term evaluation strategy can be expensive in both engineering effort and time. Take long-term holdbacks as an example: they require supporting two separate machine learning model variants in production over an extended period—one for the original control experience and another for the new, potentially more performant version based on these short-term A/B test results. This setup can quickly become complex and difficult to manage.

Second, if the product team isn't likely to roll back a change or make meaningful decisions based on long-term insights, the additional effort can feel unnecessary. When the cost outweighs the perceived value, teams often deprioritize these evaluations.

In other words, teams often avoid running longer-term evaluations because the engineering costs seem to outweigh the benefits. While this is a valid concern, other equally compelling reasons exist to invest in measuring long-term impact, such as the following:

- Uncovering delayed effects
- Preventing misleading short-term gains or degradations
- Capturing cumulative or compounding effects

This is why long-term impact measurement matters: some product changes take time to show their full value—or, in some cases, their drawbacks. For example, a new feature might only have a small immediate effect but could significantly improve retention over time. Similarly, infrastructure improvements, like faster website loading times, may quietly boost user retention in ways that only become clear after extended observation. By focusing on long-term evaluations, you can uncover these gradual yet meaningful effects that short-term tests might overlook.

On the flip side, short-term wins don't always translate into long-term success. For instance, a feature that increases user engagement initially might lead to user fatigue or frustration over time if it's too intrusive, like overly aggressive notifications. Or a pricing promotion could boost sales in the short term but train users to only buy during discounts, ultimately hurting revenue. Without strategies like degradation holdbacks, these long-term drawbacks could go unnoticed.

For these reasons, evolving your experimentation practices to better support long-term evaluations is crucial. It ensures that your product decisions are informed by a full picture of both the immediate and lasting effects of changes. Let's quickly introduce the different strategies for measuring long-term impact before we explore them in depth and discuss how you can reduce the cost of incorporating them into your experimentation practices.

Varying Strategies for Measuring Long-Term Impact

The easiest thing you can do to measure long-term impact is to run an A/B test for a longer duration. The longer your A/B test is, the less likely it will lead to insights that may include novelty or seasonality effects. However, some practical considerations for not running tests for a long duration are the engineering complexity, potential for production incidents, and testing space availability constraints.

When running an A/B test for a long period, gating the feature launch to derive long-term impact isn't a realistic option. You can implement other strategies to measure the impact of your product features after the initial A/B testing phase. In this chapter, we'll review the following methodologies:

- Long-term holdbacks
- Post-period analysis
- Continuous monitoring
- Models predicting long-term impact

Each strategy has advantages and disadvantages, which we'll explore throughout this chapter. For example, maintaining a long-term holdback can be complex from an engineering perspective, leaving you vulnerable to an invalid holdback on a long-enough timeline. A strategy, such as continuous monitoring, as a complement to long-term holdbacks, can be employed if you have the data collection infrastructure to support observing trends and patterns over the long timeline without needing a distinct holdback group.

Now that you have the list of strategies we'll explore to measure long-term effect, let's start with the most critical factor in all of this—metrics.

Defining Relationship Between Short-Term and Long-Term Metrics

Short-term (feature-level) metrics can be proxies for long-term (company top-line) metrics. Before you start down the path of building up your tool kit for computing long-term impact, you should focus on short-term proxy metrics that correlate strongly with company top-line metrics such as retention. Using shorter-term metrics as proxies allows you to monitor the feature's impact more quickly and refine your strategy early on if necessary. Now, this doesn't mean you shouldn't measure long-term impact with the right evaluation strategy, such as a holdback, but it does enable you to potentially refine your product strategy early on if you find that your short-term proxy metrics aren't moving in the right direction.

Let's look at an example at MarketMax to illustrate further.

Engineer Task: Defining Short-Term and Long-Term Metric Relationship

Continuing with your role as an engineer at MarketMax who understands the importance of measuring the long-term impact of product changes, you decide it's time to define the relationship between short-term metrics and long-term customer retention. This approach will help you make faster decisions that align with MarketMax's long-term product strategy. What short-term metric would be most meaningful in defining a relationship with retention?

 Engineer Task: What short-term metric do you think would be most helpful to define a relationship with the long-term customer retention metric?

To get started, you decide it would be most meaningful to define a relationship between the add-to-cart (short-term) and retention (long-term) metrics. The add-to-cart metric establishes the percentage of users who add an item to their cart during a session, an important indicator of interest and the shopping experience of purchasing craft goods on the MarketMax website. The long-term metric, retention, measures the percentage of customers who return to make additional purchases within a specific time frame, such as 60 days. If MarketMax has high retention, it signifies strong satisfaction with the craft goods and the user experience of buying craft goods on the website.

A strong add-to-cart rate illustrates users' interest in the craft goods sold at MarketMax, suggesting they're likely to make a purchase. Improving this metric reflects potential progress in the shopping experience on the MarketMax website, which can eventually lead to more purchases and retention. On the other hand, it's worth noting that adding an item to the cart doesn't guarantee a purchase. Product experience or pricing friction points could prevent users from completing the craft good purchase transaction.

In theory, having one short-term metric would be ideal. However, in practice, using both metrics in tandem makes more sense. To get the most accurate picture of long-term retention potential, you should establish a relationship between retention and both short-term metrics, add-to-cart and purchases.

When short-term metrics are reliable proxies for long-term outcomes, product and engineering teams can confidently act on early signals, iterate faster, and align short-term actions with long-term goals, ultimately improving overall product and business health. The relationship between short-term and long-term metrics is critical because it ensures that your product strategy optimizes for what truly drives long-term business success.

Short-term proxies for long-term metrics aside, let's explore a long-term evaluation strategy, holdbacks.

Deploying a Long-Term Holdback

Supporting long-term holdbacks requires thoughtfulness, patience, and dedication to the craft. Configuring a holdback that runs for an extended period can get complex, as you must ensure that you're maintaining a valid holdback without new features that slip through the cracks, making the holdback control group invalid.

Two types of holdbacks are used to measure long-term impact: single feature and cumulative holdbacks. For a single-feature holdback, also referred to as a feature-degradation holdback, the control group only lacks an individual feature being evaluated for its long-term impact. The control group, also referred to as the holdback group, will still receive all other new features and updates that rollout during the experiment.

A cumulative holdback, also referred to as persistent or product-version holdback, includes multiple features that ladder up to either a strategic product vision or a product cycle from a planning point of view, such as a quarter. Unlike a feature-level holdback, the control group in the cumulative holdback will not receive any new features or updates during the experiment's duration. The cumulative holdback approach excludes the holdback group from all new features during the evaluation period. The holdback group remains on the "old" version of the product without any updates, serving as an accurate baseline. This allows you to observe the cumulative effect of all feature changes. See the following image illustrating the differences between a feature-level and cumulative holdback.

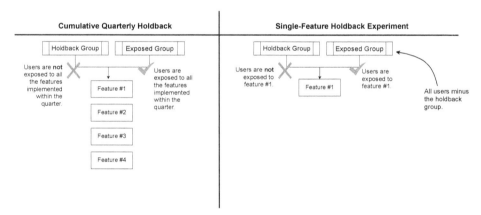

Some companies opt for a cumulative holdback to evaluate their larger product vision within their planning cycles. For instance, they may want to understand the impact on retention of all the work their engineering teams did within the past quarter. Whether you want to employ a feature-level or cumulative holdback depends on your evaluation goal. A feature-level holdback is particularly useful for isolating the impact of one specific change, while cumulative holdbacks help assess the combined effects of multiple updates released together. If you intend to evaluate a single feature, the holdback group would receive other new features and only be excluded from the one being evaluated for its long-term impact.

Now that you know two common approaches for holdbacks in product experimentation, let's explore the advantages and disadvantages in the following section.

Illustrating the Advantages and Disadvantages of Holdbacks

The advantages to employing holdbacks on your product are, of course, the fact that you will be able to measure long-term impact on metrics such as retention and churn more precisely than some of the other tactics that we'll explore later in the chapter. As long as you're executing your holdback with zero configuration errors, this methodology should accurately illustrate the long-term impact of a feature or set of features on company top-line metrics such as retention or churn. Long-term holdbacks reduce the noise caused by other changes or updates that may occur during the observation period. Because your holdback group remains on the old version of the product, you'll gain a clearer picture of the feature's impact in the context of ongoing product changes. Long-term holdbacks help you avoid overestimating short-term gains and uncover cumulative or delayed effects by enabling a reliable understanding of how features perform over time.

As for the disadvantages, a lot of engineering and process is needed to enable a holdback reliably and at scale on a product. You need to get all the details right, such as ensuring that teams are able to maintain the holdback group of users by preventing those users from being exposed to the feature evaluated for long-term impact. Similarly, configuring the holdback experiment correctly may sound simple in theory, but in practice it entails keeping parity with regards to new features for both the holdback and exposed groups to get a fair apples-to-apples comparison.

The longer your holdback duration is, the more support and thoughtfulness you'll need to ensure you've implemented a valid long-term evaluation. Let's address the complexity head-on in the following section.

Addressing the Complexity of Long-Term Holdbacks

The universal truth about long-term holdbacks is that they are complex and costly unless you've engineered your product with enabling holdbacks in mind. Maintaining a long-term holdback can be resource-intensive from an engineering and time perspective.

Sometimes, despite all your best intentions, and after considering all the details, you end up with a complicated process to support a long-term holdback. The reason configuring long-term holdbacks is complex is twofold. First, long-term holdback evaluations can have a higher burden on engineering systems to maintain multiple versions of a feature for a more extended period than it would be maintained in a shorter-term experiment. For instance, consider the case where a second version of a machine learning model leverages a distinct data set and thus requires a new data pipeline, and the training pipeline is evaluated on a longer-term timeline. The original version that leverages a different dataset for training needs to be maintained so that the model's original version (v1.1) can continue to exist in production for the holdback group. See the following image, which illustrates multiple versions of the engineering infra required to support machine learning models v1.1 and v1.2.

Single-Feature Long-Term Holdback

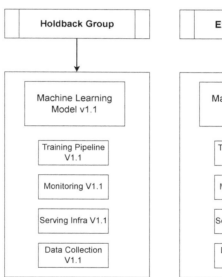
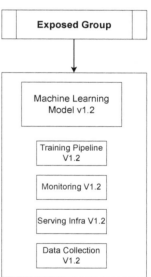

The cost of supporting a long-term holdback can include double the infrastructure, pipelines, and monitoring for **a holdback group to continue to receive the prior version** of a machine learning model, for example.

Of course, more straightforward use cases don't necessarily increase your infrastructure to support a feature-level holdback but complicate your code base by having if/else code or separate code that delineates the original version to maintain the holdback. In contrast, the new version is serving a broader user base.

The second reason for the high cost of maintaining a holdback is the difficulty of sustainably maintaining the holdback group. The users within the group are also not allocated to active A/B tests to prevent confounding factors, making it more difficult to attribute any observed differences. See the following illustration.

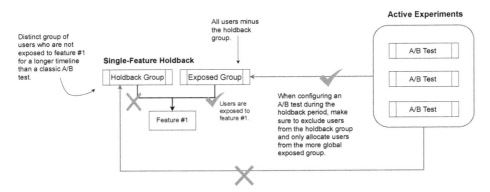

As you can see from the image, a sequence of product features is launched while a long-term holdback group is maintained for a separate evaluation. It's generally not recommended to allocate users in a holdback group to active A/B tests, especially if those tests involve changes similar to the feature evaluated in the long-term holdback. Three reasons exist why this detail is essential to maintaining the validity of your holdback group.

1. *Preserve a clean control group.* The holdback group is intended to act as a control, typically for long-term evaluation of a feature or product change. If users in the holdback group are exposed to other experiments, this can introduce confounding factors, making it difficult to attribute any observed differences solely to the feature being held back.

2. *Confounding variables.* If holdback users participate in other A/B tests, the results of the holdback experiment may be muddled by those tests. For instance, changes in a different A/B test could affect user behavior or product performance, leading to inaccurate conclusions about the impact of the holdback feature.

3. *Consistency.* The holdback group reflects a stable baseline. Allocating these users to other tests undermines that stability since they are no longer a consistent representation of the pre-feature environment.

While holdback evaluations are a prominent strategy for evaluating long-term metric impact, managing them effectively requires careful planning and consideration across not just engineering system and feature design but also the general user experience for the users in the holdback group that is frozen in time by not being exposed to new features so that the validity of the holdback is maintained. In some cases, users in a holdback group may be exposed to new features or A/B tests; those cases must be unrelated to the feature that is undergoing longer-term evaluations via the holdback. For this reason, you need to be very careful in how you maintain the holdback group over the holdback period—in some cases excluding the holdback group from the new A/B test is necessary; in other cases, it's not.

That all sounds great, but what do you think is needed in practice? Let's consider a use case at MarketMax to illustrate further.

Engineer Task: Supporting Holdbacks at MarketMax

Teams at MarketMax often leverage holdbacks to understand the effect of product changes on longer-term metrics. It's easy to support one or two holdbacks on a product, primarily if you manually ensure every day during the duration that it's configured correctly. However, it's much harder scaling and enabling many holdbacks on a product. What do you think are the key systems needed to support long-term holdbacks at scale?

 Engineer Task: What key systems and processes are needed to support long-term holdbacks at a large scale?

At a glance, here's what you need to support holdbacks at scale:

1. Clear documentation that illustrates the steps, intent, and best practices.

2. Specific tooling just for holdbacks, distinct from the general A/B testing setup.

3. Process that prevents misconfiguration of the holdback group.

Although documentation, tooling, and process are the three magic words to enable any advanced strategy in the experimentation domain, they're especially key to supporting long-term holdbacks at a larger scale.

You need clear documentation that illustrates what a holdback is, how it differs from a classic experiment, the steps to configure it, and how to monitor it over a longer time frame. Having a distinct guidebook for each area of your product is ideal, as your holdback strategy and the metrics that are measured for long-term impact may differ slightly.

By building distinct tooling to set up your holdback, you're removing the potential for misconfiguration. Remember, one of the key deterrents for running long-term holdbacks is how easy it is to misconfigure the holdback group. Misconfiguration can happen in these situations:

- You forget to enable a product feature unrelated to the holdback feature for the holdback group, preventing apples-to-apples comparison with the exposed group receiving the unrelated product feature.

- For the holdback period that could span multiple months, you let the feature slip into the product experience for the holdback group, thereby invalidating the set of users who were not supposed to see the feature until the holdback period ended.

The tool itself should have these key features:

- Ability to exclude the holdback group from a new experiment.

- Ability to quickly determine the difference between the product experience of the holdback group and the exposed group.

- Identification and listing of the features not exposed to the holdback group.

- Clear depiction of the product experience received by the holdback group.

Long-term holdbacks need tools to track how long a group has been in the holdback state and manage when they are exposed to the feature. The tool should handle different holdback durations across multiple features.

There are several reasons, a good process is critical for supporting long-term holdbacks at a large scale. Long-term holdbacks introduce complexity in implementation, maintenance, analysis, and decision-making. A well-defined process helps to ensure that these challenges can be managed effectively, especially when dealing with large user populations or multiple holdback experiments. After the holdback group receives the feature, you may still want to analyze user and product engagement metrics to see if the holdback group's long-term performance aligns with the test group. A well-structured process should also include a post-period analysis, which we'll discuss later in the chapter, to ensure that the final rollout doesn't negatively affect user experience or long-term metrics.

Here's a closer look at what MarketMax would need to increase holdback utilization in their experimentation practices:

1. *Clear documentation.* A well-documented guide specific to MarketMax's platform, detailing how holdbacks apply to its e-commerce features, including examples like personalized recommendations or home page layouts. This guide should also outline best practices, such as configuring holdbacks for seasonal campaigns, like holiday craft sales.

2. *Specialized tooling.* MarketMax would need tooling tailored for holdbacks, separate from the general A/B testing setup—for instance, a dashboard that tracks which features are excluded from holdback groups, like search features or new promotional banners.

3. *Robust process.* A seamless and straightforward process is essential to avoid misconfiguration and ensure consistent management of holdbacks—for example, automating checks to prevent unrelated features (like navigation updates or checkout optimizations) from accidentally slipping into the holdback group, or an easy method for tracking when and how the holdback group transitions to the exposed state, especially for features tied to seasonal trends or user behavior patterns, such as crafting during the holiday season.

With the right tooling, documentation, and process, MarketMax can scale its holdback approach effectively, ensuring that its insights into long-term impact remain accurate and actionable, even as the platform grows. Now that you have a firm understanding of what's needed to support long-term holdbacks at scale, let's figure out how to decrease the cost of supporting this evaluation strategy on a product by making it easier and less complex.

Reducing the Cost of Long-Term Holdbacks

How do you approach something complex—something that could potentially cause incidents, production issues, or misconfigured product experiences—and manage it effectively? You build the right tools and processes, making it hard for teams to accidentally expose the holdback group to the holdback feature or related changes. Said otherwise, your process, documentation, and tooling should make it easy to ensure the integrity of the holdback experiment is maintained.

For example, your platform tooling that enables holdback management and experimentation configuration should make it easy to validate that the holdback group is isolated from the tested feature. In practice, you would need a combination of tooling and process, such as the following:

- *Step 1.* At the start of every quarter, predefine the features for which you'd like to create holdbacks.

- *Step 2.* Around the same time, create a set of parent configurations that specific A/B tests and rollouts will inherit to honor the holdback.

- *Step 3.* As teams prepare to launch new features through rollouts and evaluate changes through shorter-term A/B tests, ensure the process includes identifying the right parent config each rollout or A/B test should inherit so that the holdback group can be maintained.

Leveraging Post-Period Analysis

Instead of maintaining a holdback group and holdback product experience, you could conduct a post-period analysis by comparing performance from before and after all users are exposed to the feature. This strategy is beneficial when the cost of maintaining a long-term holdback is impractical or too complicated.

In practice, you would conduct this analysis after the feature has been available to all users for a while, well after you've incrementally rolled it out. Instead of keeping a holdback group for an extended period and computing metrics for the smaller user population that receives the old version of the product, you analyze the impact by comparing the performance before and after the feature was launched to all users.

Timing the Post-Period Analysis

The duration you should wait before conducting a post-period analysis after launching a feature to all users depends on a couple of factors, such as the nature of the feature that's contextual to the product itself, user engagement patterns, and the long-term metrics you're analyzing.

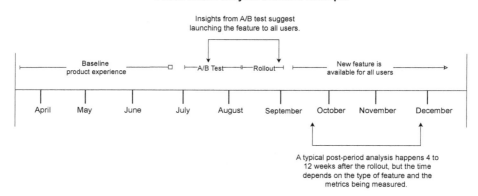

Post-Period Analysis Timeline Example

For example, suppose your objective is to measure company top-line metrics such as retention, churn, or any long-term metric. In that case, you'll need to wait eight to twelve weeks or more to conduct the post-period analysis. Or suppose your goal is to measure revenue-related metrics. In that case, you may need an even longer time window, such as three to six months, especially if you aim to identify user lifetime value metrics trends.

Comparing Benefits and Challenges of Post-Period Analysis

Post-period analysis is much less complex than a holdback from an engineering support and cost perspective. Your engineering teams have less infrastructure to manage, enabling them to allocate their time and energy elsewhere. Your business partners also benefit from this strategy—eager business partners benefit from a faster full launch, since there's no holdback group delaying broader exposure. Said otherwise, if you're in a fast-paced environment and often have pressure from your business partners, you may find post-period more appealing, as it enables the feature for all users more quickly.

However, this strategy is challenging for many reasons, including maintaining data integrity over a long period, accounting for external factors such as seasonality, and isolating the impact of the feature itself. For example, depending on the product use case, retention can fluctuate based on the time of year, making it difficult to determine whether changes in retention are due to the feature or external seasonality factors, such as a holiday or weather.

At the heart of long-term evaluations is the desire to measure top company metrics like retention; however, that requires observation over weeks or months to see the full effect of a feature. This long time frame increases the chance that other factors (like new product features, market changes, or promotions) will affect retention during the observation window, making it difficult to isolate the feature's impact.

Lastly, while one benefit of the post-period analysis strategy is that it simplifies things by avoiding the need to manage a long-term holdback, it also comes with a downside. Without a control group that consistently remains unexposed to the feature, comparisons can be less precise, and isolating the true effect of the feature becomes more challenging.

Let's see how to combat these challenges so that you can leverage the post-period strategy in your experimentation practices.

Ensuring Accurate Post-Period Analysis

The number one rule for leveraging post-period analysis is to do the up-front work before a feature is fully rolled out. The prerequisite work is to ensure you have a well-defined baseline period where user, product, and business metrics are tracked without the new feature. This data is required to compare post-rollout metric performance.

You can also leverage propensity score matching (PSM) to help control for confounding factors and create estimates for the feature's long-term causal impact. With PSM, you match users who adopted or engaged heavily with the new feature to those who didn't during a certain time period based on similar characteristics (for example, demographics and past behavior).

Although post-period analysis lacks the control group seen in long-term holdback experiments, with minimal preplanning, cohort analysis, and tools like propensity score matching, you can create reasonable approximations of the feature's long-term effect, though some residual confounding may remain. These approaches help approximate what a control group may have revealed.

While post-period analysis helps assess the sustained impact of a feature over time, it's equally important to continuously monitor user engagement after the initial launch. This allows you to track how users adopt, interact with, and return to the feature. Continuous monitoring does exactly that and complements the insights from long-term holdbacks and post-period analysis. In the following section, we'll explore this strategy in more detail.

Monitoring Impact Continuously After Feature Rollout

Let's say you want to improve your health, so you start wearing a fitness tracking watch that monitors your heart rate and steps. This watch provides real-time feedback on your performance. For instance, if you're not meeting your step goal, you might choose to walk more to reach it. After six months of using the watch and adjusting your daily exercise habits, you visit your doctor for a comprehensive health checkup to evaluate the long-term progress by measuring cholesterol levels and blood pressure and comparing your current health metrics to those from before you started.

The relationship between continuous monitoring and long-term holdbacks or post-period analysis is similar to maintaining a health regimen by monitoring day-by-day fitness through the watch and performing annual health checkups. Continuous monitoring is like using the fitness watch for day-to-day tracking, while post-period analysis and long-term holdbacks resemble the comprehensive checkup that measures sustained improvements over time.

Taking your experimentation practices to the next level involves establishing methods to monitor features after A/B test results indicate a feature rollout. While strategies such as holdbacks and post-period analysis help measure the long-term impact of a change, you also need methodologies to track the effect between the feature being launched to all users and the long-term analysis. Continuous monitoring is a strategy that fills this gap by providing insights into short-term performance, which could identify bugs that went unnoticed during the A/B test stage before final long-term conclusions are drawn.

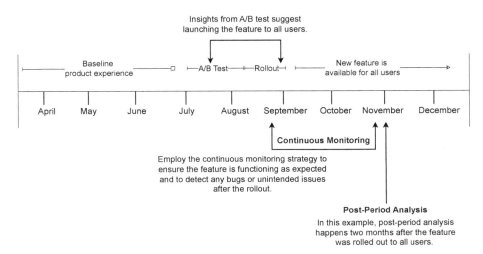

As you can see from the timeline, continuous monitoring starts once the feature is launched to all users and remains active until the post-period analysis (or holdback) can provide more comprehensive insights on the long-term impact of a feature on a product.

Complementing Holdbacks with Continuous Monitoring

The continuous monitoring strategy entails tracking performance at regular intervals over an extended period once your feature has been rolled out to users.

In practice, you would first evaluate a new feature in the form of a shorter-term A/B test. If the results suggest launching to all users, then you start enabling the feature incrementally to all users. Once the feature is fully rolled out, you start monitoring key metrics at regular intervals to observe trends or catch unexpected behavior and defects.

The most prominent challenge of the continuous monitoring framework boils down to one key question—how can you associate impact if multiple product changes are rolled out around the same time? While the continuous monitoring strategy can provide valuable product insights into how a feature performs over time, it cannot fully replace holdbacks when the goal is to measure long-term impact on critical metrics like retention, revenue, or engagement. Holdback groups serve as a control that doesn't receive the feature, which allows for direct comparison between users who experience the feature and those who don't. This clean separation helps ensure that any observed changes in the metric can be attributed to the feature. Without a holdback, it's harder to isolate the specific impact of the feature in a dynamic environment where many changes are happening simultaneously. Continuous monitoring tracks performance but may mix signals from various changes, making it challenging to draw definitive conclusions about the feature's specific impact.

That said, continuous monitoring can complement holdbacks by providing ongoing data to track trends and detect early signals, while holdbacks offer more robust, causal attribution of the feature's effect on long-term metrics. The difference here enables you to gain insights, such as in the following example. Let's say for a new feature, continuous monitoring shows an initial retention lift, but the holdback group outperforms after six months. You may notice that the feature's early gains fade over time, leading to a more refined understanding of the feature's true long-term effect.

Similarly, continuous monitoring can enable you to balance immediate adjustments with long-term learning. For instance, suppose continuous monitoring reveals that user engagement drops sharply for a specific cohort after the feature rollout. Teams can adjust the feature, but the holdback group will later verify whether these changes have improved long-term retention compared to the baseline.

Predicting Long-Term Impact with CLV Models

An additional solution to evaluating long-term impact, which cannot fully replace long-term holdbacks but can complement your strategies to measure the effect of changes made to a product, is building a model to predict customer lifetime value based on recent user engagement.

In general, predictive models can estimate long-term outcomes such as customer lifetime value (CLV) based on short-term behavior where short-term can be defined as the first 30 days of engagement. In this section we won't get into the algorithmic details of the model, but we will explore how this tactic complements the long-term holdback strategy and what it looks like in practice.

Complementing Holdbacks with Predictive Lifetime Value Models

In practice, adopting a hybrid approach is your best bet to balance speed and accuracy when evaluating long-term impact. You can utilize a predictive model to project future CLV and behavior changes early on. Then, validate these predictions through a long-term holdback to ensure the model's accuracy and capture any long-term effects the model may have failed to predict.

Said otherwise, you can use predictive CLV models to generate early estimates of long-term impact while running a long-term holdback that will take more time to derive insights but will provide a more reliable and empirical evaluation.

A hybrid approach gives you the best of both worlds:

1. You get early predictions from the CLV model.
2. You also receive reliable, empirical validation through holdback testing, ensuring the accuracy and long-term impact of those predictions.

Let's see what this looks like in practice by circling back to evaluating changes at MarketMax.

Engineer Task: Opting for a Hybrid Approach at MarketMax

A team at MarketMax has recently launched a new model that recommends craft goods to users based on their prior purchase history, and they've asked you to help them measure the long-term impact. Naturally, you opt for a hybrid approach by leveraging a predictive CLV model and long-term holdback. What is the general process for leveraging both strategies to measure long-term impact of the new recommendations model?

 Engineer Task: What is the general process for leveraging both strategies to measure long-term impact of the new recommendations model?

Assuming your trusty machine learning engineer and data scientists have already implemented a predictive CLV model based on users' behavior in the first 30 days after exposure to the new recommendation model, your first objective is to ensure a holdback group exists before any users are exposed to the new recommendations model.

For this scenario, the following holdback strategy is used:

- *Holdback group (20 percent).* Users are not exposed to the new recommendation model, serving as a control group.

- *Exposed group (80 percent).* Users receive the new recommendations model.

With 80 percent of the user base receiving the new craft recommendations on the MarketMax website, the model uses short-term engagement data from the exposed group to predict future CLV. It's worth emphasizing this key detail—that the holdback group (20 percent) serves as the control group and is not used to compute the CLV model predictions. The exposed group is used to train and generate predictions from the CLV model.

Let's assume the predictive CLV model projects that users exposed to the new craft good recommendations will have a 15 percent higher CLV over the next six months compared to the holdback group. After waiting for the duration of the holdback period (five months), you compare the actual CLV of users in the exposed group with the holdback group via the holdback analysis. The holdback analysis showed a 20 percent increase, whereas the predicted impact was 15 percent higher.

In practice, having these two complementary strategies to measure long-term impact allowed the team that built the new recommendation model to gain early insights showing the feature would have a positive impact on CLV—a metric typically outside the scope of shorter-term A/B tests. The holdback analysis ultimately validated that the true long-term impact was even higher than predicted.

Chapter Roundup: Optimizing Your Long-Term Evaluation Strategy Based on Cost

Keep in mind that the strategies you implement to improve experimentation should be practical, scalable, and tailored to what works best for your company. It's important to focus on approaches that make sense for your unique context rather than blindly following what research papers suggest works for other companies.

Every strategy in this book is rooted in the practicalities of implementing it on a real product; however, the specifics of your implementation will often depend on your company's needs and constraints. With the right combination of tooling, processes, and system design that prioritizes the enablement of holdbacks, it's entirely possible to support holdbacks at scale with reduced complexity. While holdbacks provide some of the most accurate measurements, they're just one of many tools you should have in your long-term evaluation tool kit.

Refer to the following table to compare the primary benefits and potential challenges of each long-term evaluation strategy. The right choice depends on your product and organizational needs, as each approach offers unique advantages and trade-offs.

Strategy	Primary Pitfall	Primary Benefit
Long-Term Holdbacks	Complex and engineering/process intensive to support a holdback group.	The most accurate measure of a feature's sustained effect, as they are not influenced by assumptions or short-term data patterns.
Continuous Monitoring	Not a methodology for measuring long-term impact. Lacks the ability to reveal the full long-term impact and can lead to premature conclusions if not paired with holdbacks or post-period analysis.	Real-time visibility into immediate impact, defects, or issues that weren't caught in the A/B testing stage.
Post-Period Analysis	Accounting for external factors such as seasonality, and isolating the impact of the feature itself.	If you're in a fast-paced environment and often have pressure from your business partners, you may find post-period more appealing, as it enables the feature for all users quicker.
Predicting Impact with CLV Models	There's a risk that the model may not account for external factors or shifts in user behavior, leading to inaccurate long-term predictions.	Early predictions from the CLV model, allowing you to make faster, data-driven decisions.

Wrapping Up

Great job! You've navigated the depths of measuring longer-term impact and reducing complexity with varying strategies. Without long-term measurement, you might optimize for short-term spikes that fizzle out, so having the right methodologies to monitor metrics beyond the initial A/B test is key.

Here's a quick overview of the long-term evaluation strategies discussed in this chapter:

- Long-term holdbacks provide the gold standard for measuring sustained impact but can be complex to implement at scale.

- Continuous monitoring is great for spotting immediate impacts or unexpected issues, though it won't help you understand long-term effects.

- Post-period analysis is a solid middle ground—it enables faster rollouts while still providing useful insights, but you'll need to carefully account for external factors like seasonality.

- CLV models are a powerful option, though they come with the risk of inaccuracies if the model doesn't adapt to changes in behavior or external influences.

With all the knowledge you've gained to take your experimentation practices to the next level, in the final chapter you'll explore when to make trade-offs. Should you prioritize increasing the experimentation rate or put more emphasis on improving quality? Figuring out when to prioritize improving experimentation rate, quality, and cost is just a page turn away.

CHAPTER 9

Tying It All Together

Throughout this book, we've introduced new strategies to add to your experimentation repertoire. In Chapter 8, Measuring Long-Term Impact, on page 157, we explored the various tactics to measure long-term impact beyond the classic holdback. Holdbacks are great in theory, but in practice they may be harder to implement; that's why it's critical to have other tactics available for teams to measure long-term effects.

With all these strategies in mind, you're ready to specialize and identify what you want to add to your experimentation practices so that you can enable teams to make better product decisions. In this chapter, let's take a closer look and figure out when and where to invest your time.

More specifically, we'll get into the following:

- Keeping complexity top of mind as you incorporate new experimentation tactics.

- Understanding business objectives and identifying users of the experimentation platform who aim to optimize toward those objectives.

- Deciding whether to prioritize experimentation quality versus rate.

- Operating as a data-influenced company.

It's the last chapter, so let's start with a cautionary tale of what not to do when introducing new testing strategies.

Sharing a Cautionary Tale

Picture this: a group of very smart, talented engineers on the experimentation platform team had a bold vision. They aimed to be true renegades by introducing strategies that could extract deeper insights, reduce inefficiencies, and finally tackle the dreaded bottleneck of limited testing capacity.

Just as you'd expect, the engineers started by implementing the overlapping testing strategy so that more tests could run in parallel, increasing the rate of experimentation on the product. The implementation was smooth, at least on the surface. Product engineering teams eagerly adopted the overlapping strategy, swapping out isolated test designs for overlapping experiments. But excitement quickly turned into frustration. Teams began launching experiments that were fundamentally incompatible, creating cross-experiment interference and wreaking havoc on test-result integrity. The overlapping strategy, instead of speeding up progress, was causing confusion and distrust.

Teams weren't sure which features could safely overlap. The experimentation platform engineers had unintentionally left a critical gap: they provided a powerful tool but didn't offer clear guidelines or tooling to help teams decide when overlapping tests were appropriate. What had seemed like a straightforward solution turned into a complex puzzle.

But the story didn't end there.

Around the same time, the platform team introduced covariates—a method to reduce variance and achieve more precise results with smaller sample sizes. The potential was huge, but so was the confusion. Teams struggled to identify which covariates to use and misinterpreted results. Without robust documentation, intuitive tooling, or training, the covariates addition became a source of error instead of clarity.

In the end, many teams reverted to simpler, less-effective strategies, sidelining the new more advanced strategies until better tooling and support could be provided.

This tale illustrates a really important lesson: introducing advanced strategies without proper user education, clear guidance, and accessible tools can create more problems than they solve. Even the most well-intentioned innovations can backfire if teams lack the resources to implement them effectively.

Remember that technical sophistication in your experimentation practices alone isn't enough. Your success lies in balancing complexity and usability while ensuring thoughtful practices are seamlessly integrated into the experimentation platform. In this chapter, we'll explore the common guidelines to help you avoid pitfalls similar to those in this cautionary tale so you can truly take your experimentation practices to the next level.

Building Blocks to Improve Rate, Quality, and Cost

As you've been reading this book, you may have noticed some common themes in the work required to support different experimentation strategies. For instance, improving the quality of experiments often involves building tools and infrastructure to simulate tests before they go live. This helps catch issues early and gives teams more confidence in the experiment's setup before it reaches users. Another example is the effort to increase the experimentation rate, which might involve adopting techniques like interleaving. Interleaving lets you evaluate multiple rankers within a single test variant, but it requires additional work, like shared libraries and datasets to log position and attribution for each ranker shown to users.

No matter your focus—whether it's improving experimentation rate, reducing costs, or increasing quality—the work required often falls into three fundamental categories:

- Optimization strategies
- Process improvements
- Infrastructure enhancements

Let's talk about optimization strategies first. They're the game-changing techniques that shift how teams evaluate features in a online production setting. Think about the methods we've covered in this book—random sampling, variance reduction, interleaving, multi-armed bandits, and overlapping experiments. All of these fall under the optimization umbrella. They help push experimentation to new limits while keeping your insights reliable and actionable.

Process improvements, on the other hand, focus on making it easier for teams to adopt and scale. Even small tweaks, like creating a gold standard for experiment design or developing guides on when to use more sensitive metrics, can make a big difference. These updates might seem minor, but they're essential for running experiments across an organization. Processes are never perfect, though—they'll evolve as you build better tools and adopt new strategies. You'll refine them over time, sometimes hitting the mark and other times realizing they're too clunky or slow. And that's okay! The goal isn't perfection; it's creating processes that are practical, accessible, and continuously improving.

Lastly is the infrastructure enhancement category of work. Infrastructure advancements or updates are necessary regardless of which tactic you adopt to improve experimentation rate, quality, or cost. For instance, to improve quality, you'll need to build a spot-checking tool that resembles the product experience so that teams can verify the control and test variants before launching. Or you'll surely need to make a tool that illustrates the current testing capacity and forecasted capacity so that teams can adequately plan ahead before testing traffic jams are an issue. This infrastructure category encompasses tools, systems, and frameworks that teams need to implement and scale various strategies, whether improving experimentation rate, quality, or cost.

The following Venn diagram represents the three key pillars of experimentation work—optimization strategies, process improvements, and infrastructure enhancements.

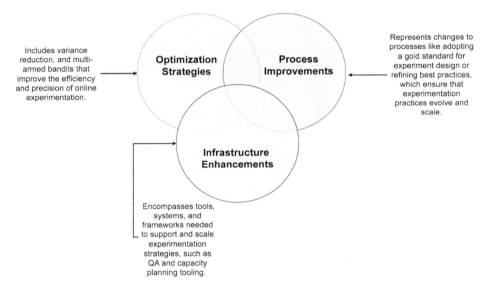

As the Venn diagram illustrates, these three pillars influence each other to drive experimentation rate, quality, and cost improvements. The overlap between these pillars emphasizes that improvements in one area often depend on or influence the others. For example, implementing an optimization strategy like multi-armed bandits requires supporting infrastructure and process updates to ensure teams can adopt it seamlessly.

Optimization strategies and process improvements often overlap when teams need clear guidelines for applying specific experimentation techniques. For example, knowing when to use variance reduction methods or interleaved experiments instead of a traditional split A/B test requires both a solid strategy and well-documented processes. Similarly, process improvements and infrastructure enhancements intersect when new tools or platforms are required to support changes—like introducing systems to verify experiments before launch to improve quality and reduce errors. Optimization strategies and infrastructure enhancements go hand in hand, as many advanced techniques rely on infrastructure upgrades. For instance, implementing adaptive testing strategies often requires building real-time monitoring capabilities to support these methods effectively.

When you're working on a product that supports large-scale experimentation, you can't really dictate how every team uses different testing methods. People will experiment in their own way—and that's okay! The best thing you can do is set them up for success by putting the right processes, tools, and optimization strategies in place. Think of it like leaving signposts along the path to guide teams as they set up experiments and race toward their product and engineering deadlines. It's all about making sure the pieces—process, infrastructure, and optimization strategies—work together seamlessly so teams can focus on what really matters: using experimentation to uncover insights.

As you reflect on which area you want to prioritize to take your experimentation practices to the next level, remember that each pillar requires some degree of process improvements, optimization strategies, and infrastructure enhancements. You can't simply create new tools without updating processes, for instance. Similarly, you can't introduce new optimization strategies without adding tools that ensure easier adoption or enablement by teams that run experiments on the product.

Understanding the Company's Strategic Goals

There may be nothing more important than understanding the broader context in which your experimentation platform operates. If your platform is disconnected from reality, then it will struggle to evolve meaningfully. For example, if the company is moving away from deploying multiple machine learning models toward a more unified model approach, then investing in interleaving experiments may no longer be the right call. Instead, it might be more impactful to double down on increasing coverage in your offline evaluation strategy.

An experimentation platform isn't just a tool for running tests; it's the glue that connects different teams—whether it's engineering, product, marketing, or design—and aligns them with the company's mission. Each team has its own priorities: boosting conversion rates, speeding up the site, or improving user engagement. However, for experimentation to truly matter, it needs to support the bigger picture and align with the company's long-term vision.

When experiments aren't connected to these goals, they risk becoming distractions. Instead of driving meaningful progress, they add noise. That's where you come in. Your job is to help teams see how their experiments fit into the broader company strategy. Whether you're working with product managers, engineers, or data scientists, it's about showing them how their work contributes to that shared "north star."

A strong experimentation platform is more than just software and system architecture; it's the foundation that supports every team's goals. It should be flexible enough to handle diverse objectives, scalable enough to keep up with demand, and consistent enough to ensure reliable and actionable results. In the end, the platform isn't just about running tests—it's about enabling smarter, faster decisions that move the company forward.

The following image illustrates how an experimentation platform serves the needs of the business, product, engineering, and other teams, enabling them to measure and achieve their objectives.

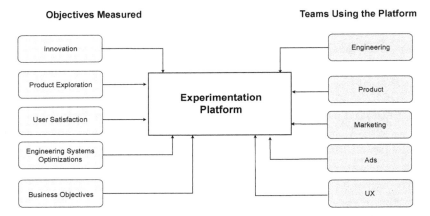

As you can see from the diagram, many teams use the experimentation platform to improve their decision-making, optimize performance, and drive results aligned with their specific objectives. You'll also see many different types of objectives, such as business-oriented and engineering system objectives.

What makes an experimentation platform truly valuable is its versatility. It needs to support a broad range of goals—whether that's driving revenue or fine-tuning infrastructure—and do so without losing sight of the bigger picture. Experimentation can't exist in a silo. To maximize the platform's potential, you need to understand what teams are trying to accomplish and how their work connects to the company's overarching mission. When done right, experimentation becomes more than just a tool for testing ideas; it becomes a strategic driver that keeps everyone gliding in the same direction.

Keeping Your Users Top of Mind

It's safe to say that you are heavily interested in online experimentation on a product. If you weren't, you wouldn't be reading the last chapter of this book! You want to understand what it takes to evolve how you evaluate changes on a product, from using the traditional split fixed-horizon A/B test to more sophisticated strategies, such as interleaving or sequential testing.

While you might enjoy digging into the finer details of experimentation, most users of the platform have a much simpler goal: they want to run an A/B test, see how their changes affect key metrics, and make a decision. That's it. They're not interested in unpacking every nuance of advanced strategies or statistical techniques—they just want results they can trust.

This is a crucial point to keep in mind as you build tools, documentation, and processes. If what you create feels too complex or burdensome, teams are unlikely to adopt it. Even the most advanced strategies won't gain traction if they're too difficult to implement. Simplicity is key—your goal is to make it easy and intuitive for teams to use the platform, no matter their level of expertise.

At the end of the day, your job is to bridge the gap between deep experimentation knowledge and the practical needs of the teams relying on it. By focusing on usability and clear guidance, you can make advanced strategies accessible and impactful.

Next, we'll explore how to balance complexity and practicality, ensuring innovation is both effective and approachable.

Balancing Complexity with Usability

While advanced experimentation strategies offer the potential for powerful insights and sophisticated analysis, implementing overly complex strategies can be counterproductive if teams need more knowledge or resources to operate them effectively. The success of an experimentation framework lies not only in its technical capabilities but also in how well teams understand, adopt, and use it to drive decision-making. Even the most innovative strategies will only deliver value if they are manageable for product and engineering teams to adopt and maintain.

Complex strategies also require robust infrastructure to support them. For example, implementing sequential testing or adaptive experiments might involve real-time data streaming, dynamic traffic allocation, and frequent metric updates. If the experimentation platform isn't equipped to handle these requirements—or if teams don't fully understand how to configure the tools—the result can be unreliable experiments, wasted resources, and an erosion of confidence in the experimentation process.

The key to successful experimentation lies in striking a balance between complexity and accessibility. While it's essential to expand the experimentation tool kit to include advanced strategies, these should be adopted incrementally and only when they address a specific need. The rollout of such strategies should also include a focus on education, user-friendly tools, and supporting processes to ensure that teams can confidently leverage them.

Before implementing a new experimentation strategy or framework, consider these elements:

- Learning curve
- Complexity and usability balance
- Scalability and impact radius

First, do teams have the tools and know-how they need to tackle a more advanced experimentation strategy without getting stuck on a steep learning curve? If not, brainstorm how can you build the right tools and platform to reduce the friction for teams that are not experts in experimentation to use the testing frameworks effectively. Strategies that require experimentation-specific or implementation-specific knowledge should be accompanied by strong onboarding and ongoing support to ensure success.

Second, is the added complexity of introducing the new strategy into your engineering and product organization's experimentation ecosystem justified? Could a simpler approach achieve the same results as the more complex strategy? If so, aim to build the simpler solution. If a complex strategy will greatly improve experimentation strategy, figure out an architecture or set of tools that make it easier for teams to adopt. For instance, if you're implementing adaptive testing, provide visualization tools that show traffic allocation in real-time or create templates for common configurations to reduce decision fatigue for teams.

Finally, can this strategy be scaled and standardized across teams, or is it too niche to be widely adopted? If only a small slice of the larger experimentation pie can leverage the new strategy, then it may not be worth implementing for such a small subset of use cases.

Considering Your Experimentation Platform's Robustness

It all starts with a clear understanding of where your platform exceeds and where your platform falls short. As you're building out new approaches to evaluate the impact of a new feature on a product, you'll be introducing new methodologies to teams that run experiments. Your platform should be flexible to support different experiment types and capable of integrating new strategies, such as isolated, interleaved, sequential, and overlapping tests. The platform should be modular, allowing teams to plug in new components or metrics as needed.

Additionally, your platform should be easy to use for all teams, regardless of their level of technical expertise. So, irrespective of the innovative strategies you build to enable deeper and quicker insights, adoption will lag if your platform is hard to use. Investing time into creating more user-friendly interfaces and tools that ensure teams can leverage the platform without friction is essential. For instance, you could consider building easy-to-use templates for common experiment types.

Comparing Experimentation Cost Versus Quality

As you evolve your experimentation practices, one crucial consideration is finding the sweet spot between quality and cost. High-quality experiments are the gold standard—they deliver precise, actionable insights that teams can trust when making product decisions. But let's be real: achieving this level of rigor often comes with a price tag in terms of tools, time, and engineering support.

On the flip side, slashing costs by spending less time or resources on experiment setup can backfire. Cutting corners might result in unreliable data or misleading results that hinder, rather than help, decision-making. The challenge is striking the right balance: how can you ensure meaningful outcomes without overburdening your teams?

Consider this: running a large-scale A/B test with a properly sized sample to ensure statistical rigor may take longer to configure and analyze, requiring more resources up front. While this approach enhances quality, it also increases the time and cost of experimentation. Conversely, opting for smaller sample sizes or shorter test durations might lower costs but could lead to less reliable or incomplete insights, leaving you with questions rather than answers.

The key is knowing when to prioritize high-quality setups and when a faster, leaner approach is appropriate. Not every experiment needs to be designed to perfection, but the ones that drive significant business decisions or product changes likely should be. By empowering teams with clear frameworks and tools to navigate these trade-offs, you ensure that experimentation remains a powerful, efficient tool for innovation and decision-making.

While running high-quality experiments is often the gold standard, in some situations faster, lower-cost experiments are the better approach. Not every experiment needs to achieve the highest level of precision, especially when the goal is to explore ideas quickly or gain early directional insights. For instance, smaller test-to-learn experiments—where the stakes are low and the business impact is minimal—can often be run with smaller sample sizes and shorter durations. Similarly, in the early stages of product development, when designs and concepts are still evolving, quick, low-cost experiments provide valuable guidance without overinvesting resources.

The key is to strike the right balance between cost and quality. Teams using the experimentation platform should have strategies and tools that empower them to make intentional trade-offs based on their goals. For high-impact decisions, investing in well-powered, rigorous experiments ensures reliable insights. On the other hand, for exploratory or low-stakes tests, teams can afford to optimize for speed and cost.

By enabling teams to differentiate between when they need statistically significant results and when a lighter-weight approach is sufficient, you allow experimentation to become a more efficient and adaptable process. Ultimately, it's about providing the right frameworks and guidance so teams can prioritize their resources effectively while still learning and iterating at a meaningful pace. Your role as an experimentation leader is to enable the act of experimenting, and having many tools in your tool kit can support balancing quality, speed, and cost in a way that aligns with specific goals. When teams have the flexibility to choose the right approach for their needs—whether it's a quick exploratory test or a robust, high-stakes evaluation—you empower them to make informed decisions and maximize the value of experimentation across the organization.

Combating the "Too Costly" Myth

At some point, you may encounter individuals who argue that running A/B tests is too costly or disruptive to the user experience. They might claim that withholding features from certain users during an experiment will erode trust in the product. This is what we call an experimentation fallacy—a misconception that fails to account for the broader benefits of experimentation.

Consider this: companies with millions of users, like Netflix, Google, and Amazon, run many experiments daily. Yet these products remain widely used by their users. Ask yourself, as a user of these products, would you unsubscribe or stop using them simply because an A/B test was conducted? It's unlikely. Admittedly, you're part of a biased group since you're invested in improving experimentation practices—but even so, the reality remains that well-designed experiments rarely undermine user trust.

The critical point to address is that labeling experimentation as "too costly" reflects a miscalculation overlooking the long-term benefits that come from improving experimentation on a product. By refining how you enable an A/B test—through better tooling, streamlined workflows, and more efficient designs—teams can maximize insights while minimizing resources. The perceived cost of experimentation pales in comparison to the value it delivers in driving informed product decisions.

It's also worth noting that A/B testing isn't a perfect methodology, but it remains the most rigorous and reliable option for measuring the true impact of a change. Other approaches, such as launching a feature to 100 percent of users and monitoring metrics through observational analysis, may seem simpler, but they come with serious trade-offs. Without a proper control group, it becomes nearly impossible to distinguish correlation from causation. Was the lift in conversion due to the new feature, a marketing campaign, a seasonal trend, or some other external factor? You're left guessing. In contrast, a well-designed A/B test provides a clear counterfactual, isolating the effect of the change with statistical rigor. No other method offers the same theoretical guarantees for estimating unbiased uplift.

Increasing Experimentation Rate Is a Balancing Act

Running more experiments on a product is undeniably appealing, especially when space capacity issues cause delays. A higher experimentation rate enables faster learning, quicker iterations, and the chance to explore more ideas at once. However, it also comes with its own challenges that need thoughtful attention.

First, when adopting the overlapping testing strategy, be cognizant of interaction effects or cross-experiment interference. For instance, two overlapping experiments modifying similar parts of the user interface could create a combined effect that skews results. To mitigate this risk, you can implement tooling that actively monitors for interactions between experiments. Such tools could flag potential conflicts in real time, allowing teams to adjust configurations or isolate experiments as needed to preserve result integrity. Let's say experiments A, B, and C launch simultaneously. The tool would monitor for cross-experiment interference and flag potential conflicts or overlapping features. Teams that own the experiments would decide whether the concern for interference is valid and if so, restart the test but with an isolated test design.

Second, while focusing on increasing experimentation rate, create the space in your roadmap to improve experimentation quality. Running more experiments at the expense of quality can lead to unreliable insights, wasted resources, and erosion of trust in the experimentation platform. This involves designing experiments with proper statistical rigor, maintaining consistent metrics definitions, and implementing monitoring systems to track experiment health throughout their life cycle. A high experimentation rate only delivers value when the results are actionable and reliable.

Third, as experimentation rate increases, managing testing capacity becomes a critical challenge. Not every experiment needs to run simultaneously, nor should it. Introducing a prioritization framework can help teams identify which experiments are most critical to the product or business. Build tools that allow teams to tag experiments by impact level, urgency, or strategic alignment. For instance, high-impact experiments tied to product launches or revenue goals should take precedence over lower-impact tests, such as small UI changes. Visualization tools can further aid prioritization by offering a clear view of current and upcoming experiments, ensuring that capacity constraints are managed effectively.

Operating as a Data-Influenced Company

Let's step back and look at the bigger picture: experimentation isn't just about optimizing features or validating ideas—it's the backbone of a data-influenced company. We use the term data-influenced intentionally because "data-driven" is overused and often not practiced as deeply as it's preached. In reality, every company—no matter how much they champion being data-driven—will face situations where opinions or intuition outweigh the data.

For example, a situation may arise when a C-suite executive insists on launching a feature, regardless of what the A/B test results suggest. And that's okay, not exactly ideal, but it is okay. Being data-influenced doesn't mean data always gets the final say; it means data shapes the conversation, informs decisions, and provides a foundation for understanding impact—even when the decision veers in another direction. See the following illustration.

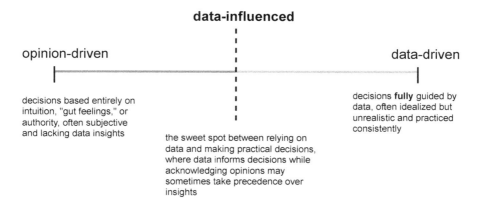

As an experimentation savant, your goal is to equip teams with the right strategies to validate assumptions, whether they come from engineers, product leads, or executives driving the roadmap. By doing so, you create an environment where decisions can be as informed as possible. If strong opinions or gut-feelings on a feature exist, your experimentation strategy enables teams to have the right data to steer opinion-heavy conversations toward more informed and balanced outcomes.

To do this, the following is involved:

- *Empowering teams with accessible tools.* Build experimentation tools that are user-friendly and reduce the complexity of setting up and running tests. Templates for common test designs, intuitive interfaces, and automation for repetitive tasks can lower barriers and encourage broader adoption of experimentation practices.

- *Educating stakeholders on experimentation principles.* Ensure that teams understand the "why" behind experimentation, not just the "how." This includes training on interpreting results, understanding statistical concepts, and knowing the limitations of A/B testing. By demystifying the process, you enable teams to trust and rely on data more confidently.

- *Balancing experimentation quality and speed.* Not every decision requires a perfectly powered, statistically rigorous test. Teach teams when it's appropriate to prioritize quick directional insights versus high-quality, precise experiments. This balance ensures that data can support both fast-paced decisions and high-stakes launches.

- *Aligning experimentation goals with company objectives.* Work closely with leadership to ensure that the experimentation platform supports the company's strategic goals. This alignment ensures that tests are not only optimizing individual features but also contributing to broader business success.

- *Providing transparency and visibility.* Build dashboards or reporting tools that make test results easily accessible and understandable across teams. When stakeholders can see the outcomes of experiments in a clear and digestible way, it strengthens trust in data and reinforces the importance of testing.

- *Iterating on the experimentation platform itself.* Just as products evolve, so should your experimentation platform. Regularly gather feedback from teams, identify pain points, and adapt the platform to meet changing needs. This continuous improvement ensures that the platform remains a valuable resource for the organization.

The result of implementing these strategies is an organization where data doesn't dictate every decision but consistently informs and influences the choices teams make as they iterate on the product.

How to Evaluate a New Strategy

Let's take a moment to imagine what it might look like to introduce one of the strategies from this book at your job. For this example, we will use interleaving.

The first step is to identify a few opportunities within your product that you can leverage interleaving to evaluate rankers. Once you've pinpointed those use cases, implement the necessary interleaving library and datasets and integrate interleaving minimally to enable these initial experiments. Running multiple use cases will give you enough experience to form a strong opinion—either interleaving is a valuable addition to your experimentation practices or it's one of those strategies that sounds great in theory but doesn't work for your particular product area.

While the engineering team is working on implementing these initial interleaving experiments, it's also a good idea to create a decision framework to help determine whether interleaving should be platformized. For example, you could evaluate it based on these criteria:

1. Experimentation design
2. Engineering complexity
3. Product need

Let's start with experimentation design. Does interleaving improve experimentation velocity and reduce costs? For instance, if your initial experiments show that interleaving allows you to measure key engagement metrics using 40x fewer users, that's a big win! It means you're freeing up testing capacity, which is a clear benefit from a design perspective.

As for engineering complexity, your early experiments should reveal whether interleaving is too complex to implement or can be simplified to work seamlessly. Remember, a strategy that's too difficult to debug or maintain won't improve your experimentation practices.

Finally, does your product have enough ranking use cases to justify implementing interleaving? If it's only relevant to a small set of product features, then it might not be worth the effort to fully productionize.

By prototyping, running initial experiments, and using a decision framework to assess the value proposition, you can confidently decide whether to incorporate this strategy into your experimentation tool kit. This thoughtful approach ensures you're adopting the right methods to take your experimentation practices to the next level.

Revisiting Experimentation at MarketMax

You've come a long way in exploring how to take our experimentation practices to the next level, and MarketMax has been our trusty example along the way. With MarketMax's shift toward a machine learning–driven product strategy, the need to improve their experimentation practices was critical to supporting the overall business. Referring back to Chapter 1, Why Experimentation Rate, Quality, and Cost Matter, on page 1, we examined workshop insights conducted by the experimentation platform team to identify areas for improvement when running A/B tests on the product. Here's a quick recap of the key challenges they faced:

1. *Streamlining experiment configuration and validation.* Teams were spending too much time on manual QA processes, running into delays and misconfigurations.

2. *Addressing testing space constraints.* The platform often couldn't support the number of concurrent experiments needed, forcing prioritization conflicts.

3. *Reducing misconfigured and inconclusive tests.* A significant number of experiments were either aborted or yielded inconclusive results, wasting time and resources.

4. *Improving experimentation rate.* Experiments frequently experienced delays or extended timelines, which slowed down product innovation and decision-making.

Sound familiar to the experiences of running A/B tests at scale at your job? If so, that's no surprise! These challenges aren't unique to MarketMax—any company running A/B tests at scale is bound to encounter similar hurdles as they grow.

You've addressed these challenges head-on with strategies and Engineer Tasks aimed at overcoming the biggest roadblocks when practicing experimentation on a product. By introducing tooling and automation, you streamlined the setup, validation, and QA processes, making it easier to ensure experiments are properly configured before launch. Advanced techniques like overlapping test design and variance reduction strategies helped make smarter use of limited testing capacity. You also standardized QA processes, increased observability for active experiments, and equipped teams with better gold standard guidelines, empowering them to use the experimentation platform with confidence.

So, as we wrap up, take a moment to reflect on these approaches and how they can be applied to your own work. MarketMax's story is just one example. What's your company's next step in improving the practice of running A/B tests on a product?

Chapter Roundup: Tying It All Together

Experimentation is both a tool and a mindset. While it serves to achieve specific goals, it also promotes a culture of continuous learning and data-influenced decision-making. It's not just about reaching an end but about fostering a process that guides product development and innovation. To guide product and engineering teams, you need a sophisticated set of tools, processes, and algorithms to enable deeper insights with ease.

As you continue to implement new tactics to make it easier or better for teams to measure the effect of changes made to a product, here are some factors to always consider, perhaps serving as guiding stars toward the path to improving your experimentation practices:

- Prioritize experimentation quality if the company aims to pivot its product strategy and take big bets. In these scenarios, precise and reliable data is critical to make informed decisions that could shape the company's trajectory.

- Manage experimentation costs and increase the rate of testing by enabling teams to run experiments with fewer users. Techniques like interleaving, metric sensitivity analysis, or other strategies detailed in this book can help optimize traffic allocation without sacrificing result reliability.

- Prioritize experimentation quality if teams often end tests early or misconfigure experiments from a statistical and product-validity perspective. Build in safeguards, such as prelaunch validation tools, statistical rigor checks, and experiment-monitoring dashboards, to minimize errors and maximize confidence in results.

- Optimize your experimentation efforts for the teams that use the platform. Make sure the tools and processes are simple and intuitive so that each new strategy is successfully adopted. Even the most advanced experimentation tactics will fail to deliver value if they are too complex for teams to understand or implement effectively.

Finally, always keep the company's strategic goals in mind so that you align all your experimentation efforts and roadmap with the larger objectives. Experimentation should serve as a bridge between individual team objectives and the organization's overarching mission. Keeping these goals in mind ensures that your roadmap is always relevant and impactful. This way, you can confidently say that your experimentation platform can support driving the business and product forward.

Wrapping Up

We've explored a wealth of experimentation concepts together! Because you chose to read this book, it's clear that you're committed to making a meaningful impact on how teams evaluate the effectiveness of the features and changes they introduce to a product. Experimentation is more than just a tool—it's a mindset, a discipline, and a catalyst for growth.

This chapter brought together the critical elements that drive experimentation forward:

- Understanding your company's strategic goals is essential for shaping an experimentation roadmap that delivers both tactical insights and long-term impact.

- Balancing complexity, scale, and usability ensures that experimentation strategies remain accessible and practical for teams while delivering meaningful results.

- Prioritizing quality, speed, and cost helps frame and navigate trade-offs, ensuring that experimentation serves as a reliable guide for decision-making at all levels.

Experimentation isn't a static process; it's a dynamic and evolving practice. Each new method, tool, or insight builds on the last, unlocking opportunities to innovate. Success in experimentation comes not from chasing perfection but from fostering a culture of continuous improvement—a culture where teams feel empowered to test and learn. As you embark on the next stage of your experimentation journey, remember: the real power of experimentation lies not just in the data it generates but in the decisions it informs. It's about creating a framework where teams can confidently explore, iterate, and make choices that drive the product and the business forward.

Now take what you've learned in these pages to elevate your experimentation practices to the next level, harnessing advanced strategies with practicality. Happy experimenting!

Index

Thank you!

We hope you enjoyed this book and that you're already thinking about what you want to learn next. To help make that decision easier, we're offering you this gift.

Head on over to https://pragprog.com right now, and use the coupon code BUYANOTHER2025 to save 30% on your next ebook. Offer is void where prohibited or restricted. This offer does not apply to any edition of *The Pragmatic Programmer* ebook.

And if you'd like to share your own expertise with the world, why not propose a writing idea to us? After all, many of our best authors started off as our readers, just like you. With up to a 50% royalty, world-class editorial services, and a name you trust, there's nothing to lose. Visit https://pragprog.com/become-an-author/ today to learn more and to get started.

Thank you for your continued support. We hope to hear from you again soon!

The Pragmatic Bookshelf

Pragmatic Bookshelf

SAVE 30%!
Use coupon code
BUYANOTHER2025

Practical A/B Testing

Whether you're a catalyst for organizational change or have the support you need to create an engineering culture that embraces A/B testing, this book will help you do it right. The step-by-step instructions will demystify the entire process, from constructing an A/B test to breaking down the decision factors to build an engineering platform. When you're ready to run the A/B test of your dreams, you'll have the perfect blueprint.

Leemay Nassery
(166 pages) ISBN: 9798888650080. $29.95
https://pragprog.com/book/abtest

Programming Machine Learning

You've decided to tackle machine learning — because you're job hunting, embarking on a new project, or just think self-driving cars are cool. But where to start? It's easy to be intimidated, even as a software developer. The good news is that it doesn't have to be that hard. Conquer machine learning by writing code one line at a time, from simple learning programs all the way to a true deep learning system. Tackle the hard topics by breaking them down so they're easier to understand, and build your confidence by getting your hands dirty.

Paolo Perrotta
(340 pages) ISBN: 9781680506600. $47.95
https://pragprog.com/book/pplearn

Creating Great Teams, Second Edition

People are happiest and most productive if they can choose what they work on and who they work with. Self-selecting teams give people that choice. Build well-designed and efficient teams to get the most out of your organization, with step-by-step instructions on how to set up teams quickly and efficiently. This new edition highlights ten years of additional insights, real-world case studies, and adaptations for remote and hybrid environments. Learn from the successes and challenges faced by organizations worldwide as they implemented self-selection, and discover a practical roadmap to unlocking team potential and fostering a culture of autonomy and engagement.

Sandy Mamoli and David Mole
(180 pages) ISBN: 9798888651339. $43.95
https://pragprog.com/book/mmteams2

Agile Web Development with Rails 7.2

Rails 7.2 completely redefined what it means to produce fantastic user experiences and provides a way to achieve all the benefits of single-page applications—at a fraction of the complexity. Rails 7.2 integrated the Hotwire frameworks of Stimulus and Turbo directly as the new defaults, together with that hot newness of import maps. The result is a toolkit so powerful that it allows a single individual to create modern applications upon which they can build a competitive business. The way it used to be.

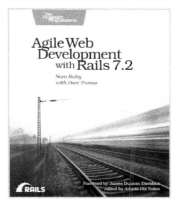

Sam Ruby
(472 pages) ISBN: 9798888651049. $67.95
https://pragprog.com/book/rails72

Business Success with Open Source

Free and open source software (FOSS) is everywhere and is the driving force behind nearly all software developed today. It doesn't matter what industry your company is in: Learning more about how to use, contribute to, and release FOSS can be the strategic edge that your company needs. With the proper knowledge and approach, open source can form the cornerstone of a digital transformation effort, increase developer retention, decrease recruiting cycles, ensure reliable security, and reinforce the company brand. All this and more, by shifting your company's FOSS strategy from accidental to intentional.

VM (Vicky) Brasseur
(470 pages) ISBN: 9798888650493. $53.95
https://pragprog.com/book/vbfoss

Guiding Star OKRs

Tired of traditional OKRs that stifle innovation and demotivate teams? The Guiding Star OKR framework offers a refreshing new approach to goal setting, emphasizing purpose, unified direction, and adaptability. Best-selling author Staffan Nöteberg distills knowledge from diverse industries, teaching you to create a compelling "Guiding Star" vision that inspires, aligns, and empowers teams. Learn to foster intrinsic motivation, embrace continuous adaptation, and unlock strategic agility for sustainable success in today's ever-changing business world.

Staffan Nöteberg
(176 pages) ISBN: 9798888651285. $42.95
https://pragprog.com/book/snokrs

Real-World Event Sourcing

Reality is event-sourced; your mind processes sight, sound, taste, smell, and touch to create its perception of reality. Software isn't that different. Applications use streams of incoming data to create their own realities, and when you interpret that data as events containing state and context, even some of the most complex problems become easily solvable. Unravel the theory behind event sourcing and discover how to put this approach into practice with practical, hands-on coding examples. From early-stage development through production and release, you'll unlock powerful new ways of clearing even the toughest programming hurdles.

Kevin Hoffman
(202 pages) ISBN: 9798888651063. $46.95
https://pragprog.com/book/khpes

tmux 3

Your mouse is slowing you down. You're juggling multiple terminal windows, development tools, or shell sessions, and the context switching is eating away at your productivity. Take control of your environment with tmux, a keyboard-driven terminal multiplexer that you can tailor to your workflow. With this updated third edition for tmux 3, you'll customize, script, and leverage tmux's unique abilities to craft a productive terminal environment that lets you keep your fingers on your keyboard's home row.

Brian P. Hogan
(118 pages) ISBN: 9798888651315. $35.95
https://pragprog.com/book/bhtmux3

The Pragmatic Bookshelf

The Pragmatic Bookshelf features books written by professional developers for professional developers. The titles continue the well-known Pragmatic Programmer style and continue to garner awards and rave reviews. As development gets more and more difficult, the Pragmatic Programmers will be there with more titles and products to help you stay on top of your game.

Visit Us Online

This Book's Home Page
https://pragprog.com/book/abtestprac
Source code from this book, errata, and other resources. Come give us feedback, too!

Keep Up-to-Date
https://pragprog.com
Join our announcement mailing list (low volume) or follow us on Twitter @pragprog for new titles, sales, coupons, hot tips, and more.

New and Noteworthy
https://pragprog.com/news
Check out the latest Pragmatic developments, new titles, and other offerings.

Save on the ebook

Save on the ebook versions of this title. Owning the paper version of this book entitles you to purchase the electronic versions at a terrific discount.

PDFs are great for carrying around on your laptop—they are hyperlinked, have color, and are fully searchable. Most titles are also available for the iPhone and iPod touch, Amazon Kindle, and other popular e-book readers.

Send a copy of your receipt to support@pragprog.com and we'll provide you with a discount coupon.

Contact Us

Online Orders:	*https://pragprog.com/catalog*
Customer Service:	*support@pragprog.com*
International Rights:	*translations@pragprog.com*
Academic Use:	*academic@pragprog.com*
Write for Us:	*http://write-for-us.pragprog.com*

www.ingramcontent.com/pod-product-compliance
Lightning Source LLC
LaVergne TN
LVHW081340050326
832903LV00024B/1233